A HISTORY OF GRAPHIC DESIGN

FOR RAINY DAYS

1776 ⊢—⊣ 1994

gestalten

Once upon a time,
somewhere in some country,
a boy is visiting his grandparents.
It's raining cats and dogs…

The boy is bored.
Bored, because unlike ordinary people, his grandparents don't have computer games, comic books, cable TV, or even internet. Everything is kinda dull and out-dated, and the only place in the house that seems any fun is his grandfather's office. But he doesn't quite know if he's welcome there...

10

THE INDUSTRIAL REVOLUTION

WE'RE HERE BECAUSE THIS IS WHERE GRAPHIC DESIGN AS WE KNOW IT TODAY STARTED TO TAKE SHAPE. SINCE THE DAWN OF TIME, HUMAN SOCIETY HAD USED ANIMAL OR HUMAN POWER AS THE MAIN SOURCE FOR ENERGY. BUT WHEN JAMES WATT (1736-1819) INVENTED THE STEAM ENGINE, EVERYTHING CHANGED. WITH THE RAPID DEPLOYMENT OF THE STEAM ENGINE, SOCIETY TRANSFORMED FROM AN AGRICULTURAL SOCIETY TO INDUSTRIAL SOCIETY. FACTORIES EMERGED AND MASS PRODUCTION BECAME A POSSIBILITY. CITIES GREW RAPIDLY AND THE CAPITALIST REPLACED THE LANDOWNER. WITH THIS NEW CONCEPT OF MASS PRODUCTION, WHAT WAS NOT YET NAMED GRAPHIC DESIGN REALLY BEGAN TO DEVELOP.

BOOKS COULD BE PRINTED IN LARGE NUMBERS, NEWSPAPERS BECAME SOMETHING EVERYONE COULD AFFORD, AND NEW TECHNIQUES FOR PRINTING PACKAGE DESIGNS AND POSTERS BECAME AVAILABLE. THIS WAS THE NEW AGE OF INFORMATION AND THAT INFORMATION WAS BROUGHT TO THE PEOPLE IN PRINT. FROM THE STEAM ENGINE TO ELECTRICAL POWER AND THE INVENTION OF THE CAMERA, NEW TECHNOLOGY MADE IT POSSIBLE TO DO THINGS THAT HAD NEVER BEEN DONE BEFORE.

DON'T WORRY. WE'RE NOW IN SCOTLAND IN THE YEAR 1775 AND THE MAN IN THE WEIRD CLOTHES IS JAMES WATT, WHO IS WORKING ON HIS OWN VERSION OF THE STEAM ENGINE. THE STEAM ENGINE WAS ORIGINALLY INVENTED BY SOMEONE ELSE, BUT WATT'S IMPROVED VERSION WAS THE ONE THAT CHANGED EVERYTHING.

1820	1830	1840	1850	1860
Aluminum is discovered	The first motor engine is invented	Morse code and the telegraph is invented	The New York Times is founded	

HUMAN BEFORE INDUSTRIAL REVOLUTION

BEFORE THE INDUSTRIAL REVOLUTION

Humans relied on animals for power, while farming was the common way to make a living. People mostly lived in villages in rural areas. The majority of the products people used were made locally and news travelled slowly.

AFTER THE INDUSTRIAL REVOLUTION

With the industrialization came the factories and around them towns formed. People moved from rural to growing urban areas, to work in the new factories. Products could now be transported long distance and the capitalist replaced the landowner.

THE TYPEFOUNDER
-1825-

FUN FACT:
The first use of the name Egyptian for slab serif fonts occurred in the specimen book of Thornes type. The name probably came from the enormous interest for Egyptian culture and all things Egyptian that was prominent in England at the time. French and German foundries later adopted the term and renamed it Egyptienne.

Connect the different terms for sans-serif with the person who coined the term.

William Caslon	Sans-surryphs
Thorowgood	Sans-serif
Blake & Stephenson	Grotesque
The Boston Type	Doric
Vincent Figgins	Gothics

DON'T WORRY, YOU'LL GET USED TO IT IN NO TIME. NOW WE'RE IN ENGLAND AND IT SEEMS TO BE AROUND 1795. THIS IS THE TYPEFOUNDRY OF VINCENT FIGGINS. YOU SEE, DURING THE INDUSTRIAL REVOLUTION IN ENGLAND, THERE WHERE THREE MAYOR TYPEFOUNDERS: WILLIAM CASLON IV, ROBERT THORNE, AND VINCENT FIGGINS.

FIGGINS IS THE MAN OVER THERE – ONE OF THE MOST SUCCESSFUL TYPEFOUNDERS OF THIS ERA. THE THREE OF THEM WERE IN FIERCE COMPETITION REGARDING WHO COULD MAKE THE BEST TYPEFACES AND TRIED TO OUTDO EACH OTHER WITH NEW ORIGINAL TYPEFACES. THEY APPLIED ALL KINDS OF DEC-ORATIONS TO THEIR ALPHABETS, WHICH RESULTED IN NEW KINDS OF TYPE LIKE FAT FACE ANDEGYPTIAN. FIGGINS HAS LATER BEEN CREDITED FOR INNOVATIONS LIKE THREE-DIMENSIONAL FONTS AND ANTIQUES/EGYPTIENNES.

WILLIAM CASLON IV INVENTED THE SANS-SERIF TYPE IN 1816, BUT THIS KIND OF TYPEFACE DID NOT SEE WIDE USE UNTIL THE EARLY TWENTIETH CENTURY.

AND WHERE ARE WE NOW? EVERYTHING HERE LOOKS REALLY OLD AS WELL. I THINK I'M GETTING TIME TRAVEL-SICK!

The lithography printer was invented by Aloys Senefelder in 1796. He discovered that instead of etching images into stone and metal, you could use an oil based crayon to write directly on the stone plate. His idea was simple: grease and water don't mix. The illustration is drawn on the flat stone surface with a greasy tool, like a crayon, and then water is applied over the stone to moisten it, making the area that is not drawn on wet while the greased drawing repels the water. Then ink is applied to the stone, adhering only to the dry area. The stone is now ready for print. Later, in 1837, the French printer Godefroy Engelman patented chromolithography. With chromolithography, the printer could separate the colours into a series of printing plates and print them one by one on top of the same sheet of paper. This made a huge impact, especially for designers. With this colourful new printing method, posters, magazines, and postcards could really capture the sentimentality, nostalgia, and idealized beauty of the era. Common things that were printed with this new technique were pictures of children, maidens, puppies, flowers, and religious motives during the Victorian era.

How to make your own lithography:

1. The image is drawn into the stone in reverse for direct printing.

2. The image and stone is damped with water and the excess removed.

3. An inked roller is worked to and fro over the damped surface.

5. The tympan is lifted and the print removed from the stone.

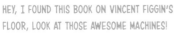

HEY, I FOUND THIS BOOK ON VINCENT FIGGIN'S FLOOR, LOOK AT THOSE AWESOME MACHINES!

Scraper

Register

Tympan of sheet metal or leather

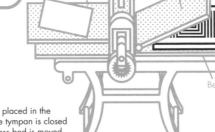

Bed

4. Paper is placed in the register, the tympan is closed and the press bed is moved under the scraper.

Mergenthaler LINOTYPE

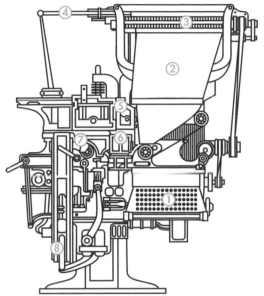

On July 3, 1886, the 32-year-old inventor Ottmar Mergenthaler demonstrated his keyboard-operated machine in the office of the New York Tribune. He had then struggled for over a decade to develop and perfect his typesetting machine. While witnessing the finished automatic typesetting machine, the editor of the Tribune Whitelaw Reid exclaimed: "Ottmar, you've done it! A line o' type!". The name stuck.

"Ottmar, you've done it! A line o' type!"

The Linotype revolutionized typesetting. In newspaper publishing, it was now possible for a relatively small number of operators to set type for many pages on a daily basis. Before Mergenthaler's invention, no newspaper in the world had more than eight pages and books were exclusive objects.

1 Keyboard 2 Magazine 3 Distributor 4 Elevator
5 Space band box 6 Assembler 7 Mold disk 8 Vise

FUN FACT: ETAOIN SHRDLU is a nonsense phrase that sometimes appeared in print in the days the linotype ruled the newspaper world. When the linotype operators made a typing error, they had to run their hand down the keyboard in order to fill in the rest of the line with letters, because single letters could not be removed, only full lines. Sometimes this went unnoticed and the nonsense phrase would appear in the newspaper. A documentary of the last linotype-composed issue of the *New York Times* is titled "Farewell, Etaoin Shrdlu".

IN 1825 A FRENCHMAN NAMED JOSEPH NIÉPCE WAS EXPERIMENTING WITH HIS CAMERA OBSCURA, A DEVICE THAT ARTISTS USED TO TRACE OBJECTS VIEWED THROUGH A LENS. CAMERA OBSCURA MEANS "DARK CHAMBER" IN LATIN AND ITS PRINCIPLE IS SIMPLE: A DARK BOX WITH A SMALL OPENING OR LENS AT ONE END LETS LIGHT PASS THROUGH IT AND THUS WHATEVER THE LENS IS AIMED AT IS PROJECTED AGAINST A GLASS PLATE ON THE OTHER SIDE OF THE BOX. NIÉPCE EXPERIMENTED USING METAL PLATES COVERED WITH LIGHT-SENSITIVE ASPHALT THAT HARDENED WHEN EXPOSED TO LIGHT. HE USED THE PLATES TOGETHER WITH A CAMERA OBSCURA AND AFTER EXPOSING THEM TO LIGHT HE WASHED THEM WITH LAVENDER OIL TO REMOVE THE PARTS NOT HARDENED BY THE EXPOSURE. HE MANAGED TO CAPTURE SOMETHING WITH THESE PLATES, THIS HAD NEVER BEEN DONE BEFORE! UNTIL THEN IMAGES HAD TO BE DRAWN OR PAINTED, BUT THE INVENTION OF PHOTOGRAPHY CHANGED EVERYTHING AND HAS PLAYED AN IMPORTANT ROLE IN GRAPHIC DESIGN EVER SINCE.

The product names are all mixed up. Match the content to the correct package.

SUNLIGHT TOBACCO — Less labour greater comfort

R.A. PATTERSON PRODUCTS CO. **ALMONDS** RICH'D, VA

All Sweet Toasted **SOAP** from California

A. Soap   **B.** Almonds   **C.** Tobacco

Eat the Victorian way! Cut out the two designs in the back of the book and apply them to your favourite jar of jam!

Even though the colourful chromolithography technique was very popular, it wasn't suitable for printing on tin cans. But an Englishman named Mr. Barkley patented the process of printing reversed images onto thin paper, which were then transferred onto a sheet of metal under pressure. And thus the classic tin can design was born.

HELLO THERE, MY FAIR LADY! ARE YOU IN NEED OF ANY ASSISTANCE?

TIHI

That darn kid broke the last stone for Prang's greeting card! Go to the back of the book and cut out the puzzle and glue it back to-gether. And while you're at it, why not colour it as well?

WE ARE NOW IN BOSTON AND THAT MAN OVER THERE IS MR. LOUIS PRANG. HE'S THE MOST INFLUENTIAL CHROMOLITHOGRAPHER OF THIS AGE. HE ARRIVED IN BOSTON A COUPLE OF YEARS AGO FROM GERMANY, AND NOW OPERATES A PRINTING WORKSHOP WITH JULIUS MAYER CALLED L. PRANG & COMPANY. THEY ESTABLISHED IT IN 1860. BACK IN THE DAYS THEY WERE DOING VERY GOOD BUSINESS PRINTING GREETING CARDS. PEOPLE WERE CRAZY ABOUT THEM IN THOSE DAYS. THE MOST POPULAR MOTIVES WERE FLOWERS, BUTTERFLIES, SMALL CHILDREN, AND OTHER ANIMALS. THE PRINTS WERE VERY REALISTIC, WHICH WAS NOT SURPRISING CONSIDERING THE FACT THAT SOMETIMES MORE THAN 40 DIFFERENT STONES WERE USED FOR A SINGLE PRINT. EVENTUALLY, PEOPLE STARTED TO REFER TO MR. PRANG AS THE FATHER OF THE AMERICAN CHRISTMAS CARD.

OWEN JONES
In the 1850s

DO NOT TOUCH THAT, YOU LITTLE RASCAL! DON'T YOU KNOW WHO I AM? I'M OWEN JONES! THE BEST PATTERN DESIGNER IN MY TIME. AND THAT, YOUNG MAN, IS ONE OF MY FINEST FABRIC DESIGNS INSPIRED BY ARABIC PATTERNS. IF YOU BEHAVE YOURSELF, PERHAPS YOU COULD HAVE A LOOK IN MY BOOK, *THE GRAMMAR OF ORNAMENT*. MANY PEOPLE REFER TO THAT BOOK AS THE DESIGN BIBLE OF THE VICTORIAN ERA. SO SINCE I'M A VERY IMPORTANT PERSON, I DON'T HAVE TIME FOR THIS NONSENSE!

ARABIC MAZE RUG!

Owen Jones travelled around the world documenting pattern designs, but this particular rug pattern seems different. Can you find your way through?

1885 — Coca-Cola goes on sale

1890 — James Naismith invents basketball

1895 — Revival of the Olympic Games

1900 — The Boer War begins

Boer War Ends

1905

STOP THAT YOU RASCAL! THAT CHAIR WAS NEARLY FINISHED!

Fill in the press name that is missing.

The Century Guild
The guild was founded in 1882. The members of the guild included potters, sculptors, designers, architects, metalworkers, and glass painters. The Century Guild's workshops produce a wide range of crafts including furniture, textiles, wallpaper, metalwork, and enamelling.

What type of animals can you find?

WE'RE NOW IN PARIS AT THE END OF THE NINETEENTH CENTURY AND THOSE TWO MEN AT THE CAFÉ ARE JULES CHERET AND EUGÈNE GRASSET. THEY ARE A PART OF A NEW MOVEMENT CALLED ART NOUVEAU, WHICH IS FRENCH FOR "NEW ART". THIS NEW MOVEMENT SEEKS TO UNITE FINE ART WITH APPLIED ARTS. THEY CONSIDER ART A WAY OF LIFE. AFTER MORE THAN TWO HUNDRED YEARS OF SECLUSION, JAPAN HAS OPENED TRADE ROUTES TO EUROPE AND A WAVE OF JAPANISM HAS FOLLOWED AS EUROPEANS ARE GETTING INSPIRED BY THE AESTHETICS OF JAPANESE PRINTS.

Art Nouveau
— PARIS —
1890

One of these posters is obviously inspired by Japanese art. But which one. And why?

LA DIAPHANE
Poudre de Riz
SARAH BERNHARDT

Art nouveau had many names. Can you match the country with the name?

Jugendstil	Austria
Sezessionstil	Netherlands
Stile Floreale	Spain
Modernismo	Italy
Nieuwe Kunst	Germany
Stile Liberty	England

SO THEY THINK THEY ARE GENIUSES, WHEN ALL THEY ARE DOING IS JUST COPYING FROM THE JAPANESE?

Art Nouveau

1890	1892	1894	1896	1898
Eiffel Tower is completed	The Tesla coil is invented	Portable typewriters are implemented	Guglielmo Marconi invents the radio telegraph	First modern Olympic games held in Greece

1900 — Marie Curie discovers radioactivity

1902 — Spanish-American War begins

1904 — First message to travel around the world

1906 — Trans-Siberian railway completed

1908

1905 Russian Revolution

HENRI DE TOULOUSE-LAUTREC

After breaking both his hips when he was 13, Lautrec became obsessed with painting and drawing. Even though he did not make more than 31 posters, he broke new ground when it came to poster design with his use of symbolic shaped and communicative images.

Colour the objects that characterized Lautrec!

SALONG DES CENT

E.GRASSET

TRUE or FALSE

~ ALFONS MUCHA ~

He was born in Czechoslovakia in 1860 but moved to Paris in 1887 to study at Académie Julian and Académie Colarossi, and later work as a designer.

It was only by pure luck that he became successful. The talented actress Sarah Bernhardt wanted a new poster for her show and Mucha was the only designer left at the printer so he had to do the job. Sarah loved his poster and signed him up on a six-year contract.

When Czechoslovakia became independet Mucha moved back to his country. Mucha was one of the first to be interrogated by the Gestapo in 1939, when Germany invaded. He died a few months later because of the harsh treatment he underwent.

Mucha considered *Le Pater* his printed masterpiece and referred to it as the thing he had "put his soul into".

The lovely actress Bernhardt later became Mucha's wife. The two of them fell in love in 1891 and were married shortly after.

Mucha led the way for the floral and hair patterned graphics of art noveau.

Mucha's middle name was Maria.

TRUE   FALSE

NOW THIS IS THE WORK OF ALPONSE MUCHA, A CZECH PAINTER AND DECORATIVE ARTIST ALSO WORKING IN PARIS, PERHAPS BEST KNOWN FOR HIS IMAGES OF NAKED WOMEN. I CAN'T SEEM TO REMEMBER EVERYTHING ABOUT HIM, SO SOME OF THIS MAY NOT BE ENTIRELY TRUE.

NAKED WOMEN?!

Find 5 mistakes in this famous Mucha poster.

BRADLEY & BEARDSLEY

— In the 1890s —

THE CHAP-BOOK

On a visit to the Boston Public Library, Bradley discovered their collection of British chapbooks. These books originated in Britain as far back as the 1500s and were usually pocket-sized booklets containing entertaining stories and illustrations for the common people. They were made from very cheap paper, often illustrated with crude woodcuts, containing wide letter spacing, and mixing of roman, italic and all capital style letters. Bradley got so inspired by these books that he developed a style named the chapbook style.

Do you know the correct colours for the chapbook poster made by William Bradley in 1895? Colour the picture to the left.

MISSING!
ETHEL REED

NOT SO FUN FACT:
To the left is an image that Aubrey Beardsley made for Oscar Wilde's play *Salomé*. His works where executed in black ink, making them very stark and striking. Beardsley had a very short career because he died of tuberculosis at the age of 25.

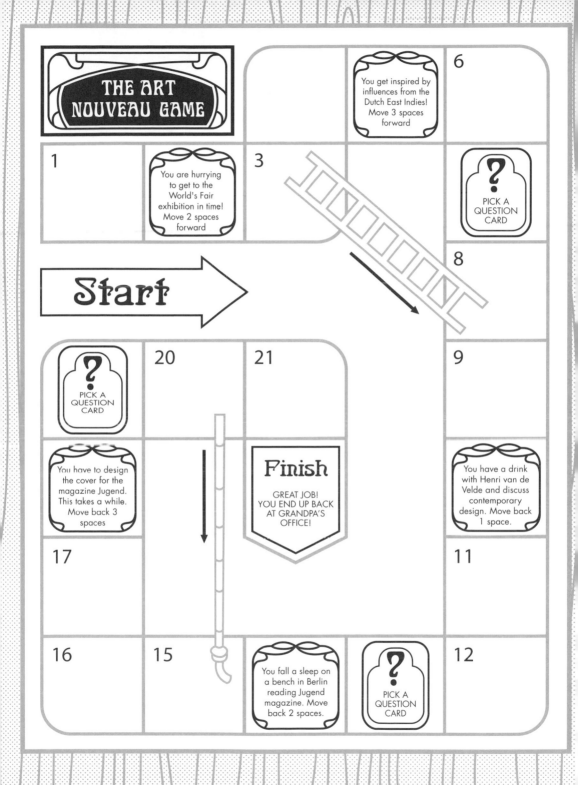

THE ART NOUVEAU GAME

6

You get inspired by influences from the Dutch East Indies! Move 3 spaces forward

1

You are hurrying to get to the World's Fair exhibition in time! Move 2 spaces forward

3

PICK A QUESTION CARD

Start

8

20

21

9

PICK A QUESTION CARD

Finish

GREAT JOB! YOU END UP BACK AT GRANDPA'S OFFICE!

You have to design the cover for the magazine Jugend. This takes a while. Move back 3 spaces

You have a drink with Henri van de Velde and discuss contemporary design. Move back 1 space.

17

11

16

15

12

You fall a sleep on a bench in Berlin reading Jugend magazine. Move back 2 spaces.

PICK A QUESTION CARD

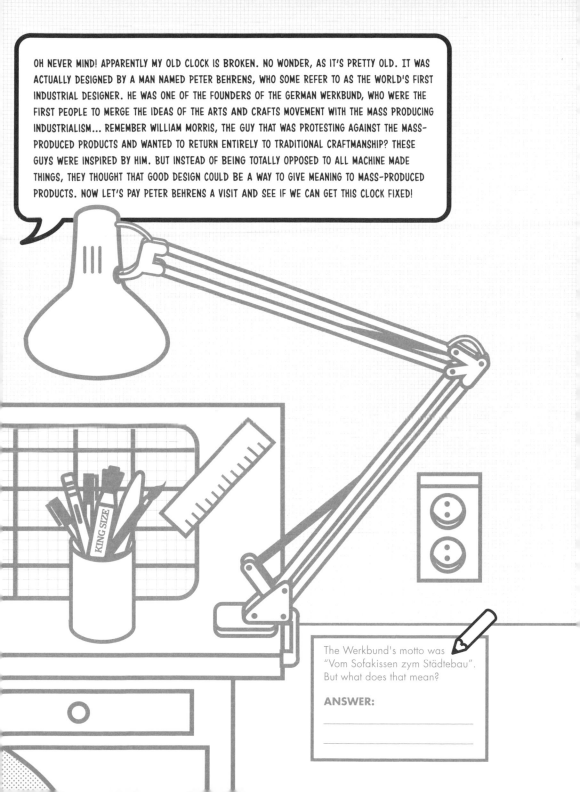

OH NEVER MIND! APPARENTLY MY OLD CLOCK IS BROKEN. NO WONDER, AS IT'S PRETTY OLD. IT WAS ACTUALLY DESIGNED BY A MAN NAMED PETER BEHRENS, WHO SOME REFER TO AS THE WORLD'S FIRST INDUSTRIAL DESIGNER. HE WAS ONE OF THE FOUNDERS OF THE GERMAN WERKBUND, WHO WERE THE FIRST PEOPLE TO MERGE THE IDEAS OF THE ARTS AND CRAFTS MOVEMENT WITH THE MASS PRODUCING INDUSTRIALISM... REMEMBER WILLIAM MORRIS, THE GUY THAT WAS PROTESTING AGAINST THE MASS-PRODUCED PRODUCTS AND WANTED TO RETURN ENTIRELY TO TRADITIONAL CRAFTMANSHIP? THESE GUYS WERE INSPIRED BY HIM. BUT INSTEAD OF BEING TOTALLY OPPOSED TO ALL MACHINE MADE THINGS, THEY THOUGHT THAT GOOD DESIGN COULD BE A WAY TO GIVE MEANING TO MASS-PRODUCED PRODUCTS. NOW LET'S PAY PETER BEHRENS A VISIT AND SEE IF WE CAN GET THIS CLOCK FIXED!

The Werkbund's motto was "Vom Sofakissen zym Städtebau". But what does that mean?

ANSWER:

WELL, I AM IN THE MIDDLE OF PRESENTING A NEW LOGO FOR THE AEG COMPANY, WHERE I SERVE AS A SO-CALLED ARTISTIC CONSULTANT. ME AND MR. RATHENAU HERE ARE DISCUSSING WHAT IS GOING TO BE THEIR UNIFIED VISUAL LANGUAGE. IF YOU JUST DECIDE WHICH ONE YOU WANT, AEG WILL BE THE FIRST COMPANY TO HAVE THEIR OWN LOGO, COMPANY TYPEFACE, AND A CONSISTENT LAYOUT ON ALL THEIR PRINTED MATTER. NOW IF RATHENAU COULD JUST DECIDE WHICH LOGO HE WANTS...

AS A VISIONARY INDUSTRIALIST I TRULY UNDERSTAND THE NEED FOR A UNIFIED VISUAL LANGUAGE FOR MY COMPANY!

Peter Behrens was born in Germany in 1868. At first he worked as a painter, illustrator and book-binder and was mostly influenced by German Jugendstil. A huge turning point in his life came when he became the second member of the Darmstadt Artists' Colony, where he as a self-taught architect, built his own house and designed everything inside it, from furniture and pottery to the paintings on the walls. In 1907 he formed the German Werkbund together with ten other artists, architects and industrialists. The same year he became an artistic consultant for AEG and for them he created what is considered the first modern corporate identity. He also designed the AEG turbine factory, as well as many of their famous products.

Do you know when the different things were invented? Write down the correct years in the different arrows...

1922   1924   1926   1928   1930

Time magazine founded   Lenin dies   Hitler publishes Mein Kampf   Pencillin discovered   Gandhi's Salt March

In 1913, Marinetti called for an typographic revolution. Classical typographic traditions and harmony were no longer a design quality. The futurists often used three or four colours and many typefaces set in both italic and bold. Expressive, dynamic, and piercing words could be given the swiftness of stars, clouds, airplanes, trains, waves, explosives, and atoms. The freedom of expression and words were born on the page. Marinetti urged poets to liberate themselves from servitude to grammar and open new worlds of expression and futurist poets threw away the constraints of horizontal and vertical structures.

Find the four futuristic items that have been scattered because of the the collision.

I THINK I BROKE SOMETHING! MY HEAD IS SPINNING!

OH YOU'LL BE ALL RIGHT! BUT LOOK WHO WE COLLIDED WITH! THIS IS FILIPPO TOMMASO MARINETTI, THE FOUNDER OF THE FUTURIST MOVEMENT.

FVTVRISM
1909–1916

Futurism was an artistic and social movement that originated in Italy in the early twentieth century. It was launched when the Italian poet Filippo Marinetti published his manifesto of futurism in the French newspaper *Le Figaro* February 20th, 1909. The manifesto expressed enthusiasm for war, machines, speed, and modern life. The public was shocked!

Embrace your inner futurist!
Cut out your very own futurist manifesto in the back of this book!

WAR POSTERS

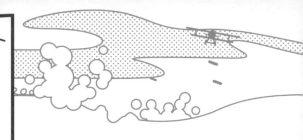

Posters were one of the most important means of public communication during the First World War. Printing technology had improved rapidly, while more advanced means of communication such as the radio was not yet widespread. The poster became important for both sides in the conflict, who used them to boost public morale and to recruit resources for the war. The visual language of the different parties in the conflict were quite different. Austria-Hungary and Germany preferred powerful shapes and patterns, unlike the Allied posters that used a much more literal and illustrative approach.

I WANNA GO TO WAR TOO! BANG BANG!

1. Who made this German poster?

Answer: _____

2. Can you fill in the missing text in the poster?

3. From which country is this poster?

Answer: _____

4. What does the text in this poster say?

Answer: _____

_____

_____

EL LISSITZKY
1890–1941

To truly understand the meaning of Russian constructivism, you have to take a closer look at one of the pioneers of this era, El Lissitzky.

Draw lines between the events in Lissitzky's life in a chronological order

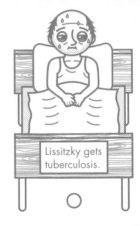

Lissitzky gets tuberculosis.

○

Lissitzky was turned down by the Petrograd Academy of Arts, because of ethnic prejudice against Jews.

○

Lissitzky and the Dadaist Hans Arp designed one of the most influencial books of its time. With the skillful use of white space, grid systems, and bold sans-serif numbers, this was an early expression of modernist aesthetics.

○

Lissitzky and the editor Ilya Ehrenburg created the journal *Veshch*, initiated by the Soviet government's official encouragement to the new Russian art.

○

Lissitzky went to Germany to study architecture at the Darmstadt School of Engineering and Architecture, which formed the basis for his art.

○

Lissitzky traveled to Berlin and the Netherlands where he made contact with De Stijl, Bauhaus, Dadaism, and other constructivists. He became an important channel, in which suprematist and constructivist ideas flowed into Western Europe.

Lissitzky was invited to join the faculty of the art school of Vitebsk in Russia. Kasimir Malevich was teaching there and became a major influence. Lissitzky developed a new painting style that he called PROUNS.

Lissitzky designed a poster for a Russian exhibition in Switzerland in which he used photomontage for complex communication messages.

LISSITZKY WAS ONE OF THE GREAT PIONEERS. HIS INDIRECT INFLUENCE WAS WIDESPREAD AND ENDURING. A GENERATION THAT MAY NEVER HAVE HEARD OF HIM STANDS UPON HIS SHOULDER.

NOW I NEED A DRINK...

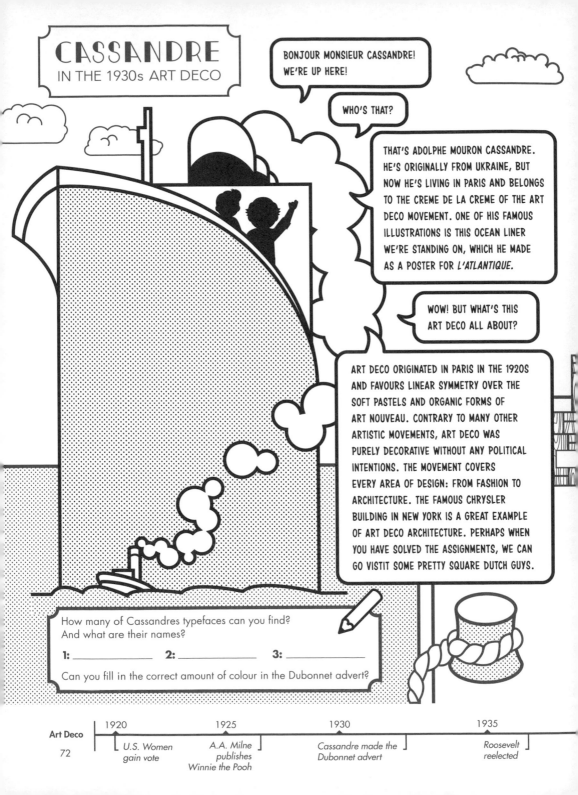

DANSE

CAFÈ
EDDY

OUVERT

CAFE

DUBONNET DUBONNET DUBONNET

1940   1945   1950   1955

World War II begins.   United Nations   Gandhi assassinated   Rosa Parks refuses to
Cassandre moves   are formed   give up her seat on a bus
to the U.S.

DE STIJL

Theo van Doesburg edited and published the *De Stijl* journal until he died in 1931. This particular issue has a cover done by Vilmos Huszár, who combines his composition with Van Doesburg's logo.

When was this particular issue published?

☐ 1916
☐ 1918
☐ 1921

MAANDBLAD VOOR DE MO-
DERNE BEELDENDE VAKKEN
REDACTIE THEO VAN DOES-
BURG MET MEDEWERKING
VA... ...NAME BINNEN- EN

WEIRD! IT LOOKS LIKE SOME OF THOSE
SQUARES ARE MISSING IN THIS COVER.
WHAT IF YOU FILL IN THE BLANKS?

bauhaus

1919 - 1933

HAVE YOU HEARD ABOUT THIS NEW THING CALLED BAUHAUS? IT'S BEEN TALKED ABOUT ALL OVER GERMANY, THESE DAYS. I'VE BEEN IN CONTACT WITH THEM, A GUY CALLED FINNINGER FROM THE BAUHAUS SCHOOL AND WE SHARE MANY OF THE SAME IDEALS ABOUT WHAT DESIGN AND ART SHOULD BE. THEY HAVE THEIR OWN SCHOOL IN WEIMAR AND I'M HOPING TO GET A TEACHING POSSITION THERE.

I'M FAMILIAR WITH THE BAUHAUS, YES. BAUHAUS WILL BE A SHORT BUT INTENSE AND IMPORTANT PERIOD FOR DESIGN IN GENERAL AND GRAPHIC DESIGN IN PARTICULAR. A LOT OF DIFFERENT PEOPLE WERE INVOLVED IN DEVELOPING THE PHILOSOPHY OF BAUHAUS AND THE THREE DIFFERENT SCHOOLS SERVED AS IMPORTANT CENTRES FOR DEVELOPING A NEW MODERNIST DESIGN MOVEMENT. IT WAS ALSO THE FIRST MOVEMENT TO CREATE A TRUE DESIGN SCHOOL ENVIROMENT.

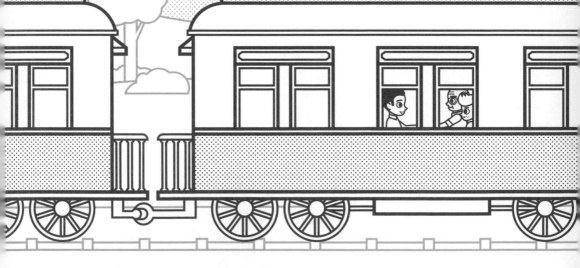

The Bauhaus Period

1918	1920	1922	1924	1926
First World War ends	The first commercial is sent on radio	Extreme inflation in Germany	The audio-movie is invented	Lenin dies

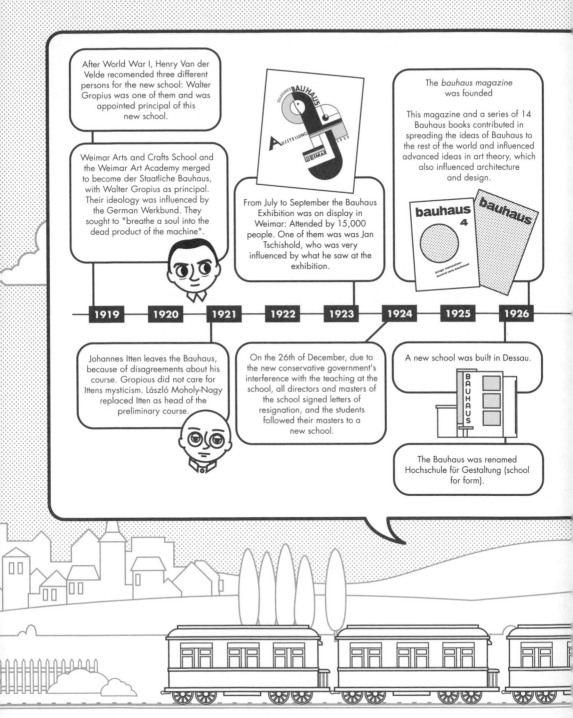

After World War I, Henry Van der Velde recomended three different persons for the new school: Walter Gropius was one of them and was appointed principal of this new school.

Weimar Arts and Crafts School and the Weimar Art Academy merged to become der Staatliche Bauhaus, with Walter Gropius as principal. Their ideology was influenced by the German Werkbund. They sought to "breathe a soul into the dead product of the machine".

From July to September the Bauhaus Exhibition was on display in Weimar: Attended by 15,000 people. One of them was was Jan Tschishold, who was very influenced by what he saw at the exhibition.

The *bauhaus magazine* was founded

This magazine and a series of 14 Bauhaus books contributed in spreading the ideas of Bauhaus to the rest of the world and influenced advanced ideas in art theory, which also influenced architecture and design.

1919   1920   1921   1922   1923   1924   1925   1926

Johannes Itten leaves the Bauhaus, because of disagreements about his course. Gropious did not care for Ittens mysticism. László Moholy-Nagy replaced Itten as head of the preliminary course.

On the 26th of December, due to the new conservative government's interference with the teaching at the school, all directors and masters of the school signed letters of resignation, and the students followed their masters to a new school.

A new school was built in Dessau.

The Bauhaus was renamed Hochschule für Gestaltung (school for form).

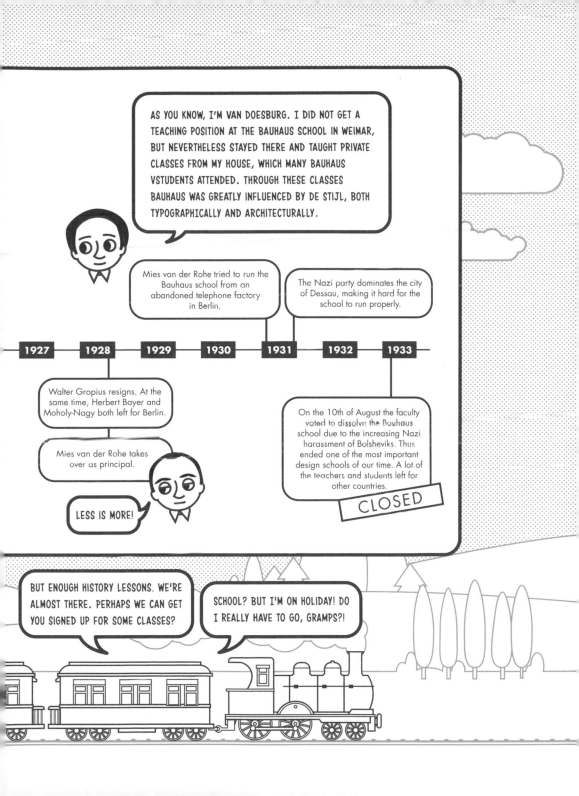

Johannes Itten's colour course

Greetings. My name is Johannes Itten. I am a painter and teacher at the preliminary course here at the Bauhaus. In my course, students learn to handle all kinds of colours, forms, and materials. I would like to share with you the knowledge of an invention of mine, I call it the *Farbkreis*, or colour wheel. From the three primary colours you should be able to create the entire wheel of different colour shades. It is really that simple.

Johannes Itten was born in Switzerland in 1888 and studied to become an elementary school teacher. In 1919 he taught at the Bauhaus in Weimar, where he developed the preliminary course that taught students about the basics of materials, composition, and colour. In 1920 he published his book *The Art of Colour*. Itten was a follower of the fire cult Mazdaznan, which he also convinced a few students into converting to. In 1923 his occultism and focus on individual artistic expression caused conflicts with Walter Gropius, who wanted to to embrace the idea of mass production. Itten resigned and was replaced by László Moholy-Nagy.

Johannes Itten

TRUE OR FALSE?

	TRUE	FALSE
Mazdaznan is a religious health movement based on Zoroastrian ideas.	O	O
The Mazdaznan followers are solely men, women are not allowed within the movement.	O	O
The Nazi party banned the practice in 1935 and this ban lasted until 1946.	O	O
It focuses on the importance of individual decision and personal responsibility for one's own fate.	O	O
Today the movement has several thousand German followers.	O	O
The movement strictly forbids sour fruits such as oranges and lemons, believing that these particular fruits are poisonous for the soul.	O	O

FUN FACT: Johannes Itten was a strict vegetarian!

HERBERT BAYER

Hello young student!

My name is Herbert Bayer. In the early days I studied painting here at Bauhaus, but later on I've founded the school's printing and advertising workshop where I now teach.

What you see here on the right is my experimental sans-serif typeface, that I've named Universal. This has been constructed solely from circles and straight lines. I want you to practice typography by designing a poster for the upcoming Bauhaus Exhibition that is going to be held here in Weimar. Design the poster based on the grid underneath and using my Universal typeface.

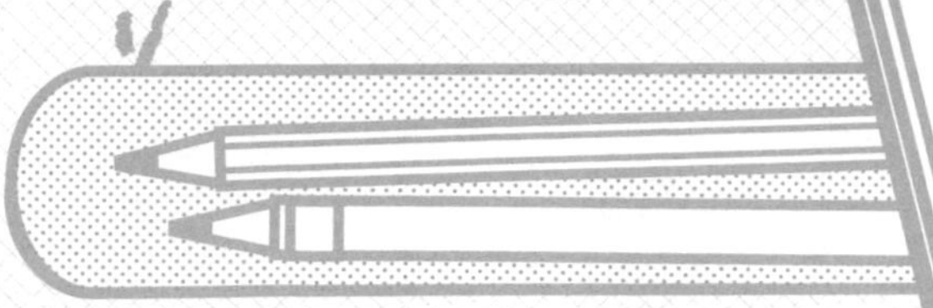

Universal typeface:

a b c d e
f g h i j k l
m n o p q
r s t u v w
x y z

EUROPÄI
-SCHES
KUNST-
GEWERBE
1927

I also designed a Dutch bank note in 1923. Can you fill in the value?

If you completed both Bayer and Itten's courses, cut out your diploma in the back of the book!

WEIMAR, DEN 9 AUGUST 1923
DIE LANDESREGIERUNG

Who made this poster?

Can you find one mistake in this painting by Kazimir Malevich?

The *Red Blue Chair* by Gerrit Rietveld needs some colour!

① Red ② Blue ③ Yellow ④ Black

JAN TSCHICHOLD & THE NEW TYPOGRAPHY

THIS BAUHAUS SCHOOL HAS HELD QUITE AN EXHIBITION, I MUST SAY. TRULY INSPIRING! THIS CHALLENGES EVERYTHING THEY'VE TAUGHT ME ABOUT TYPOGRAPHY AT THE LEIPZIG ACADEMY. YES, I FIRMLY BELIEVE THAT THIS IS THE FUTURE, THIS IS THE NEW TYPOGRAPHY AND THAT IS EXACTLY WHY EVERYONE HAS TO KNOW ABOUT THIS! WELL, ENOUGH ABOUT THAT... I'VE PUT TOGETHER A LITTLE EXHIBITION FOR YOU ON THE BATHROOM WALL. I JUST COULDN'T HOLD BACK AND IF YOU GOT THE TIME, I HAVE SOME OTHER IMPORTANT PEOPLE I WOULD LIKE YOU TO MEET. JOIN ME IN LONDON!

OH AND FORGIVE MY RUDENESS. MY NAME IS JAN TSCHICHOLD AND I AM A CALLIGRAPHER AND SIGN-PAINTER FROM LEIPZIG. IT IS A PLEASURE TO MEET YOU, YOUNG MAN!

In 1923, after visiting the Bauhaus Exhibition and with good knowledge of Russian constructivism, Tschichold was so inspired that he immediately applied their modernist ideas to his own work.

Five years later, he published his famous book *Die Neue Typographie* (The New Typography) in which he established a new set of rules for modern typography. He believed that clarity should be the main objective. He favoured headlines set to the left margin, sans-serif types, a design based on horizontal and vertical structure, and the use of photography for illustration purposes. His book set a new standard for book design, advertisements and posters.

In 1933 he escaped the Nazis, who labeled his work "un-German" and went to Switzerland, where he primarily worked as a book designer. As time went by he turned away from some of his former beliefs. Later in his life he claimed that reading a longer text set in sans-serif was genuine torture.

Later in his life, he worked for Penguin Books. He also designed the Sabon old style serif typeface, which is widely used in books to this day.

1916	1918	1920	1922	1924
The first self-service grocery store opens in the U.S.		Ghandi begins his nonviolent campaign in India	The First World War ended in November of 1918	An earthquake destroys one third of Tokyo

TSCHICOLD'S SABON

Sabon was designed by Tschichold during the period 1964–1967. The design is based on the old types of Claude Garamond, more specifically a specimen printed by a Frankfurt printer named Konrad Berner. Berner married the widow of another printer from the time, Jacques Sabon, from whom the typeface has its name. The typeface was released jointly by the Linotype, Monotype and Stempel type foundries in 1967. A revived version designed by Jean François Porchez, Sabon Next, based upon Tschichold's original design is also available.

Can you spot the Sabon?

1926	1928	1930	1932	1938
Adolf Hitler publishes Mein Kampf	A pact outlawing war is signed by 65 nations in Paris		Al Capone is sentenced to 11 years in prison for tax evasion	Germany and Japan withdraw from league of nations

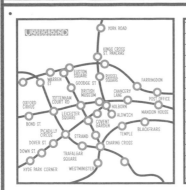

Henry C. Beck, also known as Harry beck, replaced the geographical map of the London Underground with a diagrammatical version. The London Undergrond were skeptical towards his designs, and published a small trial pamphlet in 1933, inviting public response. The response was overwhelmingly positive, and Becks topological design has since become a standard.

Based on the old map provided, create a diagrammatic subway map using these rules: Only vertical, horizontal and 45-degree lines. Different colours for each line and circles for interchanging stations. If in doubt, look up any subway map, as Beck's system is still the standard.

FUN FACT: One of Becks original maps is still preserved on the southbound platform at Finchley Central Station on the Northern Line!

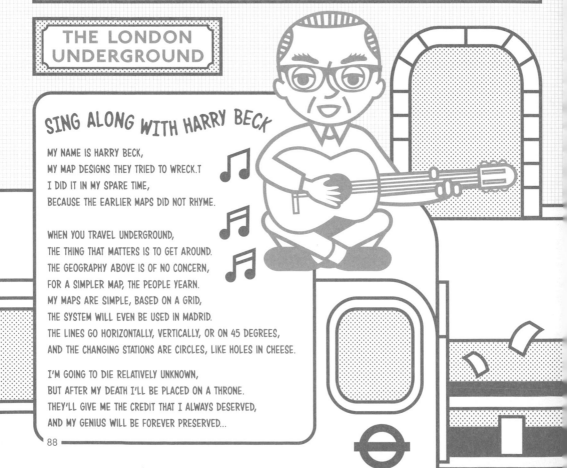

THE LONDON UNDERGROUND

SING ALONG WITH HARRY BECK

MY NAME IS HARRY BECK,
MY MAP DESIGNS THEY TRIED TO WRECK.T
I DID IT IN MY SPARE TIME,
BECAUSE THE EARLIER MAPS DID NOT RHYME.

WHEN YOU TRAVEL UNDERGROUND,
THE THING THAT MATTERS IS TO GET AROUND.
THE GEOGRAPHY ABOVE IS OF NO CONCERN,
FOR A SIMPLER MAP, THE PEOPLE YEARN.
MY MAPS ARE SIMPLE, BASED ON A GRID,
THE SYSTEM WILL EVEN BE USED IN MADRID.
THE LINES GO HORIZONTALLY, VERTICALLY, OR ON 45 DEGREES,
AND THE CHANGING STATIONS ARE CIRCLES, LIKE HOLES IN CHEESE.

I'M GOING TO DIE RELATIVELY UNKNOWN,
BUT AFTER MY DEATH I'LL BE PLACED ON A THRONE.
THEY'LL GIVE ME THE CREDIT THAT I ALWAYS DESERVED,
AND MY GENIUS WILL BE FOREVER PRESERVED...

The Johnston typeface was designed in 1916, commissioned by Frank Pick, commercial manager of the Underground Electric Railways Company of London. It was originally called Underground and later became known as Johnston's Railway Type and even later simply Johnston. The typeface is a humanist sans-serif and is based on classical roman inscriptions. Johnston used the typeface for his new Underground logo, which is still in use today. The typeface was redesigned in 1979 by Banks & Miles and this new version simply named New Johnston is the version currently used by the London Underground.

Which of these underground roundels is the correct one?

NOW WE'RE GOING TO VISIT A MAN NAMED ERIC GILL. REMEMBER TO MIND THE GAP!

FORGET THE GAP, LOOK AT THAT CRAZY TRAINSURFER!

DO NOT ATTEMPT TO ENTER A CROWDED CAR

Trains are delayed by Passengers trying to force their way into a full train. The more trains, the more costs. The shorter the stop at the station, the more trains

Train delays mean overcrowding

OFF TO THE ZOO
BOOK TO
REGENTS PARK OR
CAMDEN TOWN

VICTOR

FUTURA!

BY PAUL RENNER

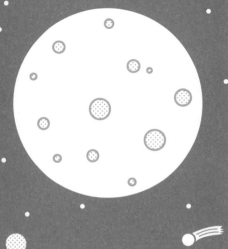

SINCE YOU'RE ALREADY LEARNING A LOT ABOUT TYPOGRAPHY, DID YOU KNOW THAT THE FIRST TYPEFACE TO EVER WALK THE MOON WAS FUTURA? NASA USED IT ON THE COMMEMORATIVE PLAQUE FOR APOLLO 11 WHICH THEY LEFT ON THAT BIG PIECE OF ROCK IN 1969. FUTURA WAS DESIGNED BY PAUL RENNER IN 1927. IT'S A GEOMETRICAL SANS-SERIF TYPEFACE AND WAS COMMISSIONED BY THE BAUER TYPE FOUNDRY. ALTHOUGH RENNER WAS NOT ASSOCIATED WITH THE BAUHAUS, HE SHARED MANY OF THEIR IDEAS ABOUT DESIGN AND TYPOGRAPHY. FUTURA WAS ORIGINALLY PUBLISHED IN LIGHT, MEDIUM, BOLD, AND BOLD OBLIQUE IN 1928, BUT LATER MORE WEIGHTS WERE ADDED. TO THIS DAY, FUTURA REMAINS ONE OF THE MOST POPULAR SANS-SERIF TYPEFACES AND HAS ALSO INSPIRED A RANGE OF OTHER SANS-SERIFS, LIKE ADRIAN FRUTIGER'S AVENIR. RENNER'S INITIAL DESIGN WAS A LOT MORE EXPERIMENTAL THAN THE FINAL VERSION, AND THESE ORIGINAL DESIGNS CAN BE SEEN IN THE TYPEFACE ARCHITYPE RENNER.

WOW! I WANT TO MOONWALK ON THE MOON, SOMEDAY!

HERE MEN FROM THE PLANET EARTH
FIRST SET FOOT UPON THE MOON
JULY 1969, A.D.
WE CAME IN PEACE FOR All MANKIND

NEIL A. ARMSTRONG
ASTRONAUT

MICHAEL COLLINS
ASTRONAUT

EDWIN E. ALDRIN, JR.
ASTRONAUT

RICHARD NIXON
PRESIDENT, UNITED STATES OF AMERICA

Do you know your Futura from your Architype Renner? Help Gramps remember how the final letter "g" turned out compared to the original, as well as how the letter "a" looked like originally?

g

a

FUTURA SAFARI

Futura is still a very popular typeface! Spend a day or two on a Futura safari and see how many different samples you can spot! Log it here, and take note of how successfully you think it is applied.

WHERE	WHAT	WEIGHT	RATING

The Second World War	1932		1934		1936		1938
	U.S. officially gets national anthem	Adolf Hitler becomes chancellor of Germany	Alcoholics Anonymous founded		Spanish Civil War	Japan invades China	The Night of Broken Glass

The International Typographic **style**

ALSO CALLED SWISS STYLE!

SO THIS IS WHERE THE GRAPHIC DESIGNERS WENT TO ESCAPE THE BAD GUYS?

BROCHMAN & CO
EDITORIAL DESIGN

THAT'S RIGHT! AND THÉO BALLMER WAS ONE OF THEM. HE STUDIED AT BAUHAUS AND TOGETHER WITH ERNST KELLER HE DEVELOPED WHAT CAN BE SEEN AS THE EARLY STAGES OF THE INTERNATIONAL TYPOGRAPHIC STYLE. THIS DIRECTION WITHIN GRAPHIC DESIGN IS ALSO KNOWN AS THE SWISS STYLE. WHAT WAS SO IMPORTANT WITH KELLER, IS THAT HE THOUGHT OF GRAPHIC DESIGN AS A DEVICE FOR COMMUNICATION AND THAT EVERY DESIGN PROBLEM HAD IT'S OWN SOLUTION WITHIN IT'S CONTEXT. TODAY THERE'S AN EXHIBITION WITH MAX BILL AND MAX HUBERT. LET'S CHECK IT OUT!

1940 | 1945 | 1950 | 1955

Japanese attack Pearl Harbor

First computer built (ENIAC)

Colour TV

Frutiger designs Univers

EXHIBITION

TYPE WORKSHOP

Features of the international typographic style:

- Use of Univers and Akzidenz Grotesk type and Helvetica.

- Use of the golden ratio and geometric grids.

- Simplification of forms.

- Photocollage and opacity.

- Influences by Tschishold's new typography style.

1960

1965

1970

The international typographic style becomes dominant throughout the world

Miedinger designs Haas Grotesque

Berlin Wall built

Malcolm X Assassinated

Che Guevara killed

max&max
EXHIBITION

Gran premio dell'Autodromo
Monza

die farbe

1

2

3

4

HELLO THERE, BOY! SO GOOD THAT YOU COULD MAKE IT TO OUR EXHIBITION. I'M MAX HUBERT BY THE WAY AND IN MY DESIGNS I OFTEN INCLUDE PHOTOMON-TAGE AND PLAYFUL USE OF OPACITY. MY WORK CAN ALMOST BE SEEN AS A COMPLEX BUT ORGANIZED CHAOS.

STANKOWSKI

1. *Answer:*
_____

LORENZ 1957

2. *Answer:*
_____

FUN FACT: Anton Stankowski was a German graphic designer, photographer, and painter. In his works, he illustrated processes or behaviours rather than objects. Through this, he developed his own unique iconography. He is also well known for his original theories on design.

HI! I JUST CAME FROM THE PRINTER AND I GOT SOME SAMPLES I WOULD LIKE YOU TO LOOK AT. CAN YOU SEE WHAT KIND OF INVISIBLE FORCE I'VE TRIED TO VISUALIZE? THE ONE ON THE LEFT IS A LOGO, THE ONE IN THE MIDDLE IS A CALENDAR COVER, AND THE ONE ON THE RIGHT IS AN ILLUSTRATION FOR A CALENDAR.

3. Answer: _____

It was Eduard Hoffman and Max Miedinger who decided to upgrade the Akzidenz Grotesk, which resulted in Helvetica. Can you do the same, by turning this Akzidenz Grotesk "a" and "y" into Helvetica? Draw the Helevtica version on top of the Akzidens version!

2

Federal income tax forms are set in Helvetica and NASA is using it on the Space Shuttle orbiter. CNN has used Helvetica as its main font for a long period, but has recently switched to Univers. Many other corporations are also using Helvetica, such as 3M, American Airlines, AT&T, BMW, Lufthansa, Microsoft, Tupperware, Toyota, General Motors, BASF, Panasonic, Nestlé and AGFA.

2

Akzidenz grotesk was made by the Berthold typefoundry between 1898-1906. It was one of the first fonts that contained a whole family of different weights. This allowed compositors to use one typeface and still achieve contrast and harmony in their layout designs.

WHAT DOES HELVETICA MEAN IN LATIN?

S _ _ _ _ _ Z _ _ _ _ _ D

What was the original name for Helvetica?

NEEU AHAS TROGEKS

....

4

Visiting
Mr. Brockmann

In 1959 the journal *New Graphic Design* was published for the first time. The editors were Carlo L. Vivarelli, R.P. Lohse, Josef Müller Brockmann, and Hans Neuburg. The magazine played an important role in the growth and unification of the Swiss design movement.

Neue Grafik
New Graphic Design
Graphisme actuel
13

FUN FACT: The movement towards developing a "world language without words" began in the 1920's. Inspired by Egyptian illustrations, the sociologist Otto Neurath believed that modern society needed a universal visual communication system. He developed a system that had the simple task to change complex information into a self-explanatory chart. His system was first called the Vienna Method, but later changed it's name to Isotype (International System of Typographic Picture Education). At first, the pictograms were individually drawn or cut out of paper by graphic artists. But then the woodcut artist Gerd Arntz joined, who from that moment on designed most of the pictograms!

SHIPPING:
Oslo, Norway

THIS SIDE UP

Can you find all the pictograms made by Neurath and Gerd Arntz? Colour or draw a blue line around all of Neuraths isotypes and use red for Arntz.

Otl Aicher designed Lufthansa's visual identity that included a special logo for the supercargo. Colour the correct version of the logo!

1: How old was Paul Rand when he started his design career?

2: Which designer almost got kicked out of Cooper Union because of "lack of talent"?

3: Who said the famous words: "Design is thinking made visual."?

1: _____

2: _____

3: _____

1960   1965   1970   1975

Brownjohn, Chermayeff & Geismar formed   *U.S. sends troops to Vietnam*   *Lubalin, Avant Garde magazine*   *Elvis found dead*

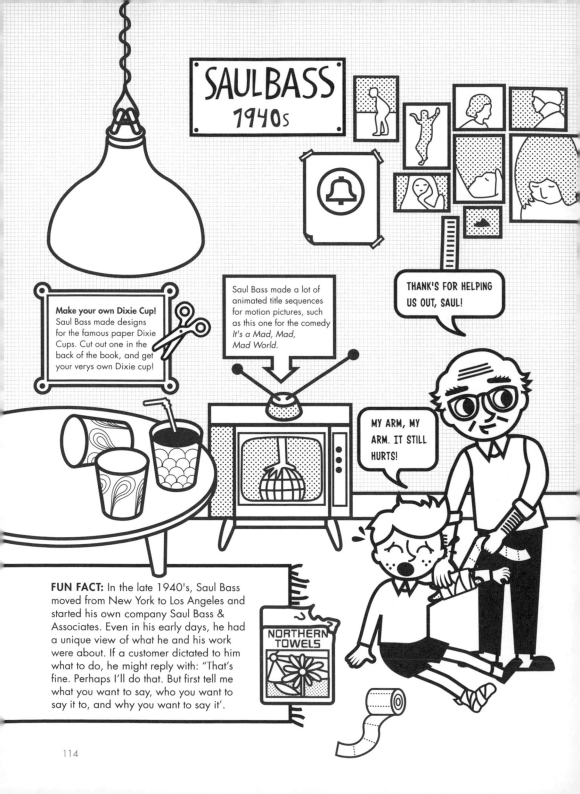

SAUL BASS
1940s

Make your own Dixie Cup! Saul Bass made designs for the famous paper Dixie Cups. Cut out one in the back of the book, and get your verys own Dixie cup!

Saul Bass made a lot of animated title sequences for motion pictures, such as this one for the comedy *It's a Mad, Mad, Mad World.*

THANK'S FOR HELPING US OUT, SAUL!

MY ARM, MY ARM. IT STILL HURTS!

NORTHERN TOWELS

FUN FACT: In the late 1940's, Saul Bass moved from New York to Los Angeles and started his own company Saul Bass & Associates. Even in his early days, he had a unique view of what he and his work were about. If a customer dictated to him what to do, he might reply with: "That's fine. Perhaps I'll do that. But first tell me what you want to say, who you want to say it to, and why you want to say it'.

NORTHERN TOWELS

When Saul Bass & Associates redesigned the Northen Paper products, their sales went up to 200%.

NO PROBLEM! BUT YOU DON'T LOOK TOO GOOD, BUDDY. LET ME READ YOU A LITTLE FROM ONE OF MY CHILDREN'S BOOKS. AFTER THAT, I WOULD ALSO RECOMMEND YOU TO CHECK OUT THE REST OF THE BUILDING. THERE ARE MANY INTERESTING PEOPLE YOU SURELY WOULD LOVE TO MEET.

"IN PARIS" SAYS HENRI. "THERE ARE THOUSANDS OF BUSES!!!"

Henri's Walk to Paris is a children's book illustrated by Saul Bass and written by Leonore Klein in 1962.

Do you recognize this arm? Which movie poster did Saul Bass use it in?

A. *Goldfinger*.

B. *The man with the golden arm*.

C. *The man with the golden gun*.

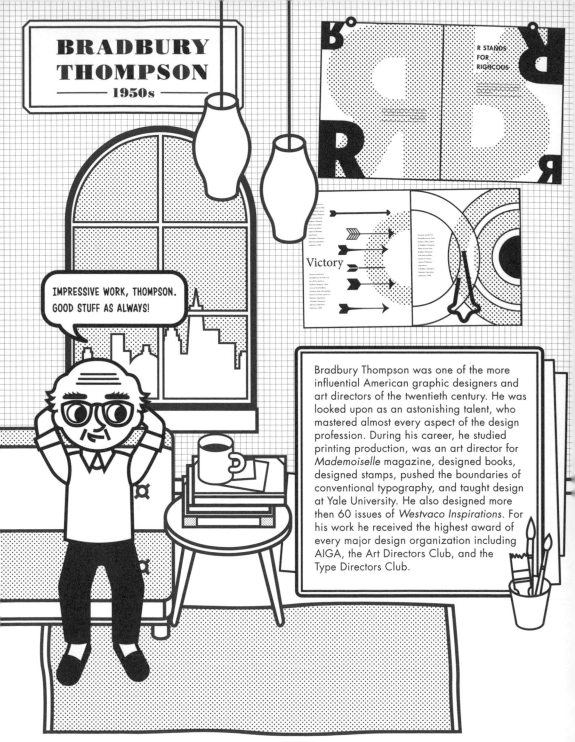

BRADBURY THOMPSON
— 1950s —

R STANDS FOR RIGHTEOUS

Victory

IMPRESSIVE WORK, THOMPSON. GOOD STUFF AS ALWAYS!

Bradbury Thompson was one of the more influential American graphic designers and art directors of the twentieth century. He was looked upon as an astonishing talent, who mastered almost every aspect of the design profession. During his career, he studied printing production, was an art director for *Mademoiselle* magazine, designed books, designed stamps, pushed the boundaries of conventional typography, and taught design at Yale University. He also designed more then 60 issues of *Westvaco Inspirations*. For his work he received the highest award of every major design organization including AIGA, the Art Directors Club, and the Type Directors Club.

Can you tell which two of these three illustrations Thompson used in his designs? Colour them!

HOWDY! AS YOU CAN SEE I'M QUITE BUSY, BUT I COULD NEED SOME HELP. COME ON IN. MY NAME IS BRADBURY THOMPSON AND I'M A GRAPHIC DESIGNER AND ART DIRECTOR. AT THE MOMENT I'M WORKING ON THE NEWEST ISSUE OF *WESTVACO INSPIRATIONS*. IT'S A PUBLICATION WAS AN INSPIRATION FOR DESIGNERS AND PRINTERS. THE WAY I WORK CONSISTS OF COLLECTING ILLUSTRATIONS, PRINTING PLATES, ARTWORKS, OLD PHOTOGRAPHS, AND LETTER FORMS AND THEN MERGE THEM ALL TOGETHER. YOU SEE; COLLECTING INSPIRES ME!

I COLLECT POKÉMON CARDS!

Make your own inspiring booklet by collecting whatever you find interesting and then merging the material together in a design to your liking.

OTTO STORCH

It began as a fourpage fashion journal entitled The Queen, but would later change its name and become one of America's leading women's magazines. In 1958, the new manager gave designer Otto Storch the opportunity to upgrade the graphics. This resulted in a fresh visual approach, where photography was unified with typography. Headlines and the magazine often became part of illustrations and the magazine was printed in a much bigger format. What is the name of this magazine?

Answer: _____

HENRY WOLF

The magazine appeared for the first time in October 1933. It later transformed itself into a more refined periodical with a focus on men's fashion. In 1953 Henry Wolf became the new art director and he redesigned the format, opening up for the use of white space and large photographs. Wolf's vision for the magazine cover was simple: a single image showing a visual idea. Which year did he became an art director for Esquire?

Answer: _____

SEVENTEEN

She was art director for Glamor, seventeen, Charm and mademoiselle. She was also the first female member at the New York Art directors Club and she made a big contribution to editorial design during the 40s and 50s in America. What was her name?

Answer: _____

ALEXEY BRODOVITCH

Alexey Brodovitch emigrated to Paris from Russia in 1920, escaping the Bolshevik's revolution. A couple of years later, he was asked to move to America to teach at the Pennsylvania Museum School of Industrial Art, which he agreed to. Soon after, he was discovered by the editor-in-chief of *Harper's Bazaar*. She knew that Brodovitch had the abilities to change the magazine into something big. He became art director at *Harpers Bazaar* and worked there for 24 years. With his bold typography, use of white space and obsessive cropping he made a major impact on the magazine's look.

Alexey Brodovitch was teaching a class of photography and graphic arts to students in New York from 1941 to 1966. He also had a selected group, which he invited to this home after class. This group consisted of students he saw had the possibilities of making something big for the printed page. He was a seer and he knew when an individual had discovered something exciting. But he had a lacking sense of empathy and could be very rude in his search for the new and seminal talents. Some of the big names that have crossed paths with Brodovitch are A.M Cassandre, Robert Frank, Man Ray, and Richard Avedon.

What was the major impact Alexey Brodovitch had on photography and magazine art direction?

Answer: _____
_____

ALEXANDER LIBERMAN

Alexander Liberman emigrated from Russia to the U.S. in 1940 and became art director at *Vogue* in 1943. He used skilled photographers such as Irving Penn, Cecil Beaton, and Lee Miller and brought new life to the magazine.

Vogue was founded by Arthur Baldwin Turnure in 1892 and is still available in several countries today. Do you know how many?

Answer: _____

1960s

"Sometimes you have to compromise legibility to achieve impact"

NOW THIS IS ONE OF THE GREATEST DESIGNERS I KNOW. HE HAS DONE A LOT OF EXPERIMENTING WITH TYPE AND IMAGES. YOU SEE, WORKING WITH TYPOGRAPHY DOES NOT ONLY INVOLVE RULES AND TRADITIONAL PRACTICE, BUT THE EXPERIMENTATION WITH CHARACTERS AND THEIR FORMS. TYPE CAN BECOME IMAGE AND IMAGE CAN BECOME A WORD OR A LETTER. ISN'T THAT WHAT YOU SAID, HERB LUBALIN?

Something is missing in these designs. Can you fill in the correct details?

Amongst his many contributions to the world of graphic design, Lubalin's magazine designs stands out as perhaps the most impressive. In collaboration with Ralph Ginzburg, he made a lot of beautiful and creative layouts for magazines like *Eros*, *Fact*, and *Avant Garde*.

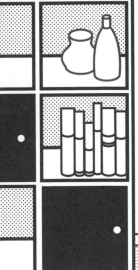

THE 50'S AND 60'S WERE THE GOLDEN AGE OF POLISH POSTER DESIGN. MOVIE POSTERS IN POLAND UNDER THE SOVIET UNION WERE QUITE DIFFERENT FROM THEIR WESTERN COUNTERPARTS. LIKE EVERYTHING ELSE, THE FILM INDUSTRY WAS CONTROLLED BY THE STATE, AND ARTISTS LIKE JAN LENIKA AND WIKTOR GORKA WHO ARE SITTING OVER THERE WERE COMMISSIONED TO DO POSTERS FOR STATE CINEMAS. THEY ENJOYED COMPLETE ARTISTIC FREEDOM TO DO WHATEVER THEY WANTED.

TWO PLEASE!

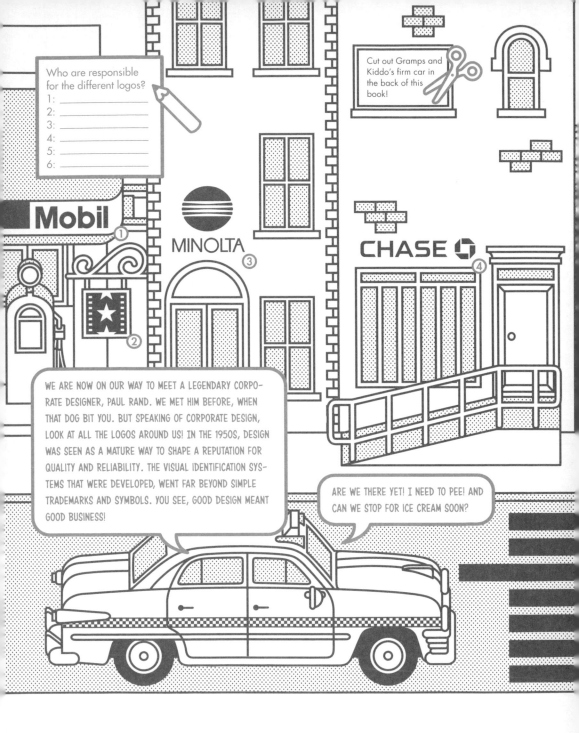

Find the right reason why Paul changed his name from Peretz Rosenbaum to Paul Rand.

A. To hide his Jewish background.
B. To have a more artistic name.
C. His twin brother had the same name.
D. The Jewish mafia was after him because of his father's involvment with the mob.

YOU'RE WORKPLACE IS QUITE DARK, PAUL. I'LL LET IN SOME LIGHT, IF YOU DON'T MIND.

Besides designing big corporate identities, Paul and his wife Ann, also worked on children's books. One of their first books was *I know a Lot of Things*, with Ann as author and Paul as illustrator.

I Know
a Lot
of
Things

Ann and Paul Rand

OOOHH! LOOK AT THAT! NOW THE LOGO ACTUALLY LOOKS MUCH MORE DYNAMIC! THE LINES UNIFY THE THREE-LETTER FORMS AND BY DIVIDING THE LOGO INTO SMALLER PARTS, IT WILL AVOID BEING POORLY COPIED BY COPIERS.

The idea of "defamiliarizing the ordinary",* which was a central concept of twentieth century art, played an important role in Paul Rand's design. By working with manufacturers, he had the opportunity to use his corporate identities to create "lively and original" packaging for ordinary items.

*An artistic technique of forcing the audience to see common things in an unfamiliar way, in order to improve their understanding of the familiar.

Which of the these logo versions did Paul Rand make?

1

2

3

4

5

6

Hint: Rand believed that a trademark should be stripped down to elementary shapes that are universal, visually unique, and stylistically timeless to be functional over a long period of time.

THE GOLD MEDAL GOES TO THE 1972 MUNICH OLYMPICS, WITH OTL AICHER AS THE LEADING DESIGNER. WITH STRICT GRIDS FOR PUBLICATION, A RADIAL SUNBURST AS AN EVENT SYMBOL, THE UNIVERS SELECTED AS TYPEFACE, AND A SET OF PICTOGRAMS OF BREATHTAKING ELEGANCE AND CLARITY, THIS PROFILE STANDS AS A MILESTONE IN THE EVOLUTION OF GRAPHIC DESIGN! OTL AICHER ALSO INTRODUCED THE FIRST OLYMPIC MASCOT, A STRIPED DACHSHUND NAMED WALDI. THIS GOLD MEDAL IS WELL DESERVED!

THE SILVER MEDAL GOES TO LANCE WYMAN'S PROFILE FOR THE OLYMPIC GAMES IN MEXICO CITY 1968. THE LOGO PERFECTLY CATCHES THE VISUAL SPIRIT OF THE TIME, WITH INFLUENCE FROM BOTH MEXICAN CULTURE AND THE OP ART OF THE 60S. WE CONGRATULATE YOU WITH SILVER!

THE BRONZE MEDAL GOES TO THE ARCHITECTURAL FIRM JERDE PARTNERSHIP AND THE GRAPHIC DESIGN FIRM SUSSMAN/PREJZA FOR THEIR WORK ON THE OLYMPIC GAMES LOS ANGELES 1984. WITH AN EXTRAORDINARY COLOUR PALETTE AND WITH THE PLAYFUL USE OF GRAPHIC ELEMENTS, THIS PROFILE IS INFINITELY ADAPTABLE. A WORTHY BRONZE MEDALIST!

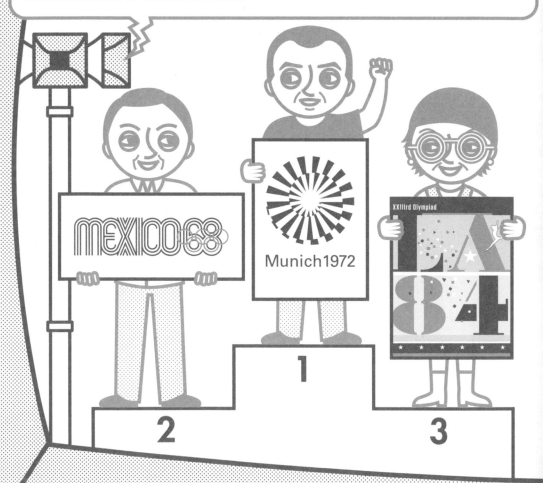

MUNICH 72 | RESULTS

Help Kiddo see which sports the results are for by finishing the pictograms.

1. John Williams (USA)
2. Gunnar Jervill (SWE)
3. Kyösti Laasonen (FIN)

1. Lones Wigger USA
2. Boris Melnik USSR
3. Lajos Papp HUN

1. Yuri Malishev (URS)
2. Alberto Demiddi (ARG)
3. Wolfgang Güldenpfennig (GDR)

1. Hennie Kuiper (NED)
2. Clyde Sefton (AUS)
3. No medal awarded

1. Csaba Fenyvesi (HUN)
2. Jacques Ladegaillerie (FRA)
3. Győző Kulcsár (HUN)

1. Reinhard Eiben (GDR)
2. Reinhold Kauder (FRG)
3. James McEwan (USA)

OH, YOU'RE WATCHING THE OLYMPIC GAMES IN MUNICH 1972! THAT'S AN EXCELLENT EXAMPLE OF HIGH-QUALITY IDENTITY WORK. THE MAN BEHIND THIS IDENTITY IS THE GERMAN DESIGNER OTL AICHER. I THINK I MENTIONED HIM WHEN WE TALKED ABOUT THE LUFTHANSA PROFILE.

YEAH, YOU DID... THE TV SIGNAL SUCKS! IT'S HARD TO SEE WHICH SPORT THE RESULTS ARE FOR!

You can cut out the manifest in the back of the book and hang it on your wall.

first
things
first

LET'S TURN OF THE TV FOR NOW, I'VE GOT SOME-THING ELSE TO SHOW YOU. THIS IS THE FIRST THINGS FIRST MANIFESTO! PUBLISHED BY KEN GARLAND IN 1964 AND BACKED BY OVER 400 GRAPHIC DESIGNERS! YOU SEE, AFTER A COUPLE OF YEARS WITH CORP-ORATE DESIGN A QUESTION AROSE ABOUT WHETHER DESIGNERS SHOULD THINK ABOUT VALUES OR NOT. THOSE WHO THOUGHT THAT VALUES WERE NEEDED, BELIEVED THAT DESIGNERS SHOULD BE MORE CRITI-CAL AND TAKE A STAND IN THEIR CHOICE OF WORK. FOR EXAMPLE: YOU SHOULD AVOID DESIGNING AND PROMOTING PRODUCTS FOR COMPANIES SUCH AS TOBACCO COMPANIES, THE WEAPON INDUSTRY AND SO ON... IT WAS A SORT OF RESPONSE TO THE CONSUMPTION CULTURE AND THE COMPANIES THAT BENEFITED FROM GRAPHIC DESIGNERS NO MATTER WHAT KIND OF PRODUCT THEY WANTED TO SELL.

THE MANIFESTO WAS UPDATED IN THE YEAR 2000, BUT I'VE GOT A PRINT HERE OF THE ORIGINAL 1964 MANIFEST PUBLICATION. GO AHEAD... TAKE A LOOK!

WHO SIGNED?

There were ?? people who signed the 1964 manifesto. Six of the following 28 people *didn't* sign. Do you know who?

Edward Wright	Georg Hammer
Geoffrey White	Ken Garland
William Slack	Anthony Froshaug
John Green	Robin Fior
Caroline Rawlence	Lindsay swanson
Ian McLaren	Germano Facetti
Christof Lara	Ivan Dodd
Sam Lambert	Harriet Crowder
Ivor Kamlish	Anthony Clift
Gerald Jones	Gerry Cinamon
Bernard Higton	Cindy Griffin
Edward Bingley	Robert Chapman
Brian Grimbly	Ray Carpenter
John Garner	Ken Briggs

NO, OUR STORY ISN'T FINISHED YET. BUT THAT BOOK YOU'RE HOLDING THERE IS ACTUALLY A STORY IN ITSELF, LET ME TELL YOU A LITTLE ABOUT PENGUIN BOOKS.

ALL THAT CORPORATE STUFF SEEMED PRETTY BORING IF YOU ASK ME. CAN'T WE TAKE A BREAK AND READ A BOOK OR SOMETHING?

PENGUIN BOOKS

PENGUIN BOOKS WAS FOUNDED IN 1935 BY ALLEN LANE, WHO HAD PUBLISHING EXPERIENCE FROM HIS JOB AS MANAGING DIRECTOR OF THE BODLEY HEAD. INSPIRED BY CHEAP READING MATERIAL HE HAD FOUND AT A TRAIN STATION, HE WANTED TO SHOW THE WORLD THAT QUALITY LITERATURE DIDN'T NEED TO BE EXPENSIVE. FEW PEOPLE BELIEVED IN HIS PROJECT, BUT THEY WERE PROVEN WRONG AND JUST TEN MONTHS AFTER THE COMPANY LAUNCHED, THEY HAD PRINTED OVER ONE MILLION BOOKS. PEOPLE LOVED CHEAP QUALITY LITERATURE!

THE PRICE FOR A GOOD BOOK IS JUST 2,5 P, THE SAME AS A PACK OF TEN CIGARETTES!

Allan Lane knew that these new cheap paperbacks had to be attractive in order to get the public's attention. Edward Young, Penguin's first production manager, did the famous original designs inspired by the earlier Albatross paperback series. The first books sported a three-part horizontal grid, with the title and author in the middle. The wordmark Penguin Books was set in faux Bodoni Ultra Bold, while the title and author was set in the relatively new Gill Sans. The books also had an identical dust cover with the price printed on it. The top and bottom field was colour coded to indicate the books subject, seperating fiction, crime, plays and so on. This clean modernist look made the books stand out in shops and was an important element in attracting new customers to buy them.

These are the ten first books Penguin published. But the titles and authors are all mixed up!

Ariel: A Shelley Romance	Compton Mackenzie
A Farewell to Arms	Mary Webb
Poet's Pub	Beverley Nichols
Madame Claire	E.H. Young
The Unpleasantness at the Bellona Club	Agatha Christie
The Mysterious Affair at Styles	Susan Ertz
Twenty-Five	Dorothy L. Sayers
William	Ernest Hemingway
Gone to Earth	Eric Linklater
Carnival	André Maurois

PENGUIN BOOKS

A FAREWELL TO ARMS

ERNEST HEMINGWAY

THE BODLEY HEAD

COMPLETE   UNABRIDGED

a Penguin Book   3/6

Nineteen eighty-four

George Orwell

In 1947–1949 Jan Tschichold was hired and made responsible for updating and refining every aspect of the Penguin Books, from logo and cover to the body text inside. He redrew Edward Youngs original logo to created a definite version and also started the development of the vertical grid design. His final rules were collected in his 4-page leaflet *Penguin Composition Rules*.

In 1961, Robert Marber designed what is referred to as he Marber Grid, initially designed for the crime series, but later applied to fiction and other genres as well. It was comissioned by Germano Facetti, the art director at Penguin at the time, to give covers more room for illustration and graphic imagery. Marber created a series of horizontal rules and used the typeface Intertype Standard (a version of Bertholds Akzidenz Grotesk) which he preferred to Helvetica.

Each genre of Penguin Books had recognizable colour schemes.
Colour the different books correctly!

What did Edward Young say when he came back from the zoo with the initial sketches of the logo?

A: Nice creatures, but they sure move around a lot!

B: My god, how those birds stink!

C: Perhaps we should have chosen the name elephant instead?

PENGUIN BOOKS

GENERAL FICTION

THE BODLEY HEAD

PENGUIN BOOKS

CRIME FICTION

THE BODLEY HEAD

PENGUIN BOOKS

TRAVEL & ADVENTURE

THE BODLEY HEAD

PENGUIN BOOKS

DRAMA

THE BODLEY HEAD

1965
Civil Rights Act
passes in U.S.

1968

1971
Woodstock Festival

1974
Terrorists attack at
the Olympic Games
in Munich

The Vietnam
War ends

1977
Elvis found
dead

NOT SO FUN FACT: Rick Griffin's left eye was dislocated in a car accident and many believe that this was the inspiration behind the famous eyeball in his work.

Cut out and build your own Volkswagen Bus in the back of the book!

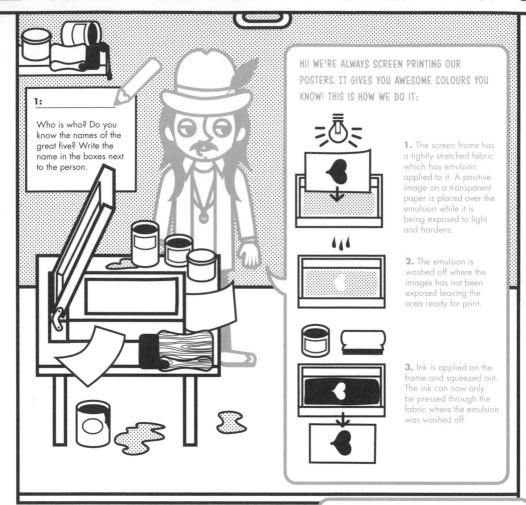

1:

Who is who? Do you know the names of the great five? Write the name in the boxes next to the person.

HI! WE'RE ALWAYS SCREEN PRINTING OUR POSTERS. IT GIVES YOU AWESOME COLOURS YOU KNOW! THIS IS HOW WE DO IT:

1. The screen frame has a tightly stretched fabric which has emulsion applied to it. A positive image on a transparent paper is placed over the emulsion while it is being exposed to light and hardens.

2. The emulsion is washed off where the images has not been exposed leaving the area ready for print.

3. Ink is applied on the frame and squeezed out. The ink can now only be pressed through the fabric where the emulsion was washed off.

2: _____

WELCOME TO THE BERKELEY-BONAPARTE DISTRIBUTION AGENCY! WE PRODUCE AND SELL PSYCHEDELIC POSTER ART. MANY OF THE POSTERS WE DO ARE FOR AVALON BALLROOM HERE IN SAN FRANCISCO. AN AWESOME PLACE WITH LOTS OF GROOVY MUSICIANS! SOME OF THE MOST FAMOUS POSTERS WE DID, WERE FOR THE GRATEFUL DEAD. THOSE WERE FAR OUT MAN!

150

HINT: This designer is known for his diverse visual language by exploring new motifs and graphic techniques. He founded *New York* Magazine in 1968 together with Clay Felker.

He made several display typefaces. These where first used only for projects and then later turned into complete typefaces.

He worked as a partner with the designer Seymour Chwast for over two decades and together they founded Push Pin Studios.

Soviets launch first
man in space

Nelson Mandela
sentenced to life
in prison

Che Guevara
killed

Yasser Arafat
becomes leader
of the PLO

U.S. pulls out
of Vietnam

ODERMATT & TISSI

1970s

HELLO THERE, YOU TWO! GLAD YOU COULD COME VISIT! WE USED TO BE A PART OF THE INTERNATIONAL TYPOGRAPHIC STYLE, BUT NOW WE ARE BORED WITH ALL THAT STRICT GRID-BASED TYPOGRAPHY. WE FEEL THAT DESIGN SHOULD HAVE PERSONALITY AND THAT, IF IT FEELS RIGHT, IT DOESN'T MATTER IF IT FOLLOWS A GRID OR NOT. OUR NEW WORK IS MUCH MORE PLAYFUL THAN WHAT WE USED TO DO. PERHAPS YOU COULD HELP ME WITH THE POSTER BEHIND ME? IT'S SUPPOSED TO SAY ENGLERSATZAG IN DIFFERENT LETTERS, BUT I CAN'T COME UP WITH THE LAST ONES. REMEMBER THAT IT'S ALL ABOUT BEING PLAYFUL!

E N L

E S

T G

e

Yale University welomes:
WOLFGANG WEINGART

GOOD DAY STUDENTS! MY NAME IS WOLFGANG WEINGART, I'M A GRAPHIC DESIGNER FROM EUROPE. I'M HERE TO TALK ABOUT MY WORK. I ALWAYS TRY TO EXPERIMENT AND PLAY WITH A LOT OF DIFFERENT TECHNIQUES. I EXPERIMENT WITH TYPOGRAPHY AND PICTURES, OFTEN IN DIFFERENT DIMENSIONAL LAYERS TO CREATE COLLAGES. SOME REFER TO MY WORK AS NEW WAVE TYPOGRAPHY, OTHERS CALL IT SWISS PUNK TYPOGRAHPHY. HERE YOU CAN SEE THREE DIFFERENT EXAMPLES OF WORK I'VE DONE. I TRY TO APPLY THE "GUTENBERG APPROACH" TO MY WORK, THAT MEANS BEING INVOLVED IN ALL THE DIFFERENT ASPECTS OF THE PROCESS LIKE CONCEPT, TYPESETTING, PREPRESS PRODUCTION, AND PRINTING TO ENSURE THE REALIZATION OF MY VISIONS. I WOULD STRONGLY ENCOURAGE YOU ALL TO DO THE SAME.

FUN FACT:
Weingart said he never intended to create a style. It just happened that students picked up —and misinterpreted—a so-called "Weingart style" and spread it around.

Where was Weingart born?
A: Germany
B: Switzerland
C: Austria

YES. A LOT OF THE EUROPEANS TRAVELED TO AMERICA TO GIVE LECTURES, AND THIS HELPED IN SPREADING POSTMODERN IDEAS. LET'S LISTEN TO THIS LECTURE AND THEN WE CAN GO VISIT A WOMAN NAMED PAULA SCHER.

I'VE NEVER SEEN ANYTHING LIKE THIS!

WHAT?! SCHOOL AGAIN?

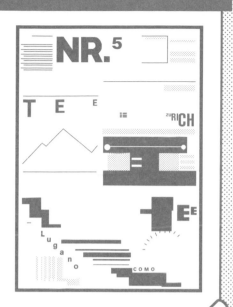

Which designer did he have as his teacher?
A: Emil Ruder
B: Armin Hoffmann
C: Paul Rand

THIS GUY SURE HAS A SUSPICIOUS ACCENT!

Gramps seems to have forgotten about these three important postmodernists. Can you help him fill in the blanks?

APRIL GREIMAN

Born:
1948
Studied at:

Taught:
Head of the design department at the California Institute of the Arts
Worked:

WILLI KUNZ

Born:

Studied at:
Kunstgewerbe-schule Zurich (School of Arts and Crafts)
Taught:

Worked:
His own design studio

DAN FRIEDMAN

Born:
1945
Died:

Studied at:
Ulm Institute of Design & Basel School of Design
Taught:

Worked:

HELLO, MY NAME IS PAULA SCHER. I WORK AS A GRAPHIC DESIGNER HERE AT CBS RECORDS. THE ONE THING I CAN'T STAND ABOUT GRAPHIC DESIGN NOWADAYS IS HELVETICA. IT'S LIKE THE MOST BORING TYPEFACE IN THE WORLD! AND I DON'T WANT TO DO BORING STUFF. LATELY I'VE BEEN DISCOVERING A LOT OF GRAPHIC DESIGN FROM THE EARLY TWENTIETH CENTURY, AND I FIND THAT MUCH MORE INTERESTING THAN ALL THIS STRICT GRID-BASED STUFF. SO THE KIND OF WORK I DO IS A LOT MORE PLAYFUL AND OFTEN DIRECTLY INSPIRED BY HISTORICAL PIECES. YOU CAN SEE SOME OF THE DESIGN I'VE DONE FOR CBS ON THE WALL HERE, PERHAPS YOU CAN FIGURE OUT WHAT I WAS INSPIRED BY?

PAULA SCHER 1980s

Can you see which design era Paula Scher was inspired by, when designing these record sleeves?

LEONARD BERNSTEIN STRAVINSKY NEW YORK PHILHARMONIC

Inspired by: _____

BEST RETURN TO FOREVER STEVE KHAN FERGUSON HUMPHREY MAHAVISHNU ORCHESTRA COBHAM HUBERT LAWS GETZ HUBBARD

Inspired by: _____

FUN FACT:
Paula divorced Seymour Chwast five years after they got married, but they remarried in 1989!

158

CROUWEL & VAN TOORN

1970'S

JAN VAN TOORN started out as a graphic designer in 1957 and focused on meaning rather than a smooth stylistic expression. He wanted the viewer to make an effort processing his design and thought that designers should think more about design's role in shaping contemporary reality. His radical teachings were highly influential on the younger generation of Dutch designers.

When were Crouwel's famous stamps for the Dutch PTT in circulation?

☐ 1976–2002

☐ 1980–2000

☐ 1978–2007

70 c nederland   45 c nederland

WIM CROUWEL was one of the founders of the design studio Total Design. He mainly focused on constructing type, always working on a grid. Crouwel is especially admired for his systematic approach and his creative handling of lettershapes.

Use the grid to finish the letters from the New Alphabet typeface!

VAN ABBEMUSEUM EINDHOVEN

CHAGALL
DUCHAMP
KANDINSKY
YVES KLEIN
MONDRIAAN
MOHOLY NAGY
PICASSO
f273969,-+

DE BEYERD

je ne cherche pas,
je troupe

MENS EN OMGEVI

ub ecd i

TO BE HONEST, THE NEW ALPHABET TYPEFACE WAS OVER THE TOP AND NEVER REALLY MEANT TO BE USED. NOW HURRY UP, VAN TOORN!

PUNK design 1970s

DURING THE BRITISH PUNK ERA A LOT OF YOUNG PEOPLE ADOPTED A DO-IT-YOURSELF MENTALITY. THEY USED BASIC TOOLS LIKE PHOTOCOPIERS, MARKERS, SCISSORS, AND GLUE TO PRODUCE ROUGH LOOKING FANZINES ABOUT PUNK MUSIC AND CULTURE. TECHNIQUES LIKE COLLAGES AND RANDOM TYPOGRAPHY, SIMILAR TO THE WORK OF THE DADAISTS, BECAME A PUNK TRADEMARK AND THIS D.I.Y APPROACH ALSO INSPIRED A LOT OF YOUNG GRAPHIC DESIGNERS.

Sniffin Glue fanzine was founded in 1976 by musician Mark Perry and ran for 12 issues over one year. The first issues only sold about 50 copies, but for the later issues, as many as 15,000 copies, were distributed. The fanzine was notorious for its hastily written and unfiltered articles, and was crucial for defining and spreading the punk ideology in England.

FUN FACT: The famous *London Calling* album by The Clash is a homage to Elvis Presley's debut album!

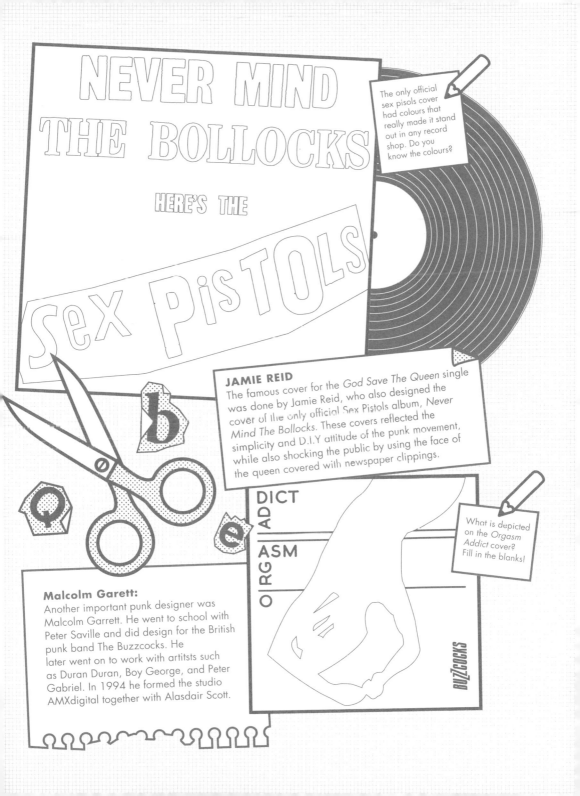

NEVER MIND THE BOLLOCKS HERE'S THE Sex PiSTOLS

The only official sex pisols cover had colours that really made it stand out in any record shop. Do you know the colours?

JAMIE REID
The famous cover for the *God Save The Queen* single was done by Jamie Reid, who also designed the cover of the only official Sex Pistols album, *Never Mind The Bollocks*. These covers reflected the simplicity and D.I.Y attitude of the punk movement, while also shocking the public by using the face of the queen covered with newspaper clippings.

DICT
AD
ASM
ORG
O

What is depicted on the *Orgasm Addict* cover? Fill in the blanks!

BUZZCOCKS

Malcolm Garett:
Another important punk designer was Malcolm Garrett. He went to school with Peter Saville and did design for the British punk band The Buzzcocks. He later went on to work with artitsts such as Duran Duran, Boy George, and Peter Gabriel. In 1994 he formed the studio AMXdigital together with Alasdair Scott.

AT FIRST I STUDIED FINE ART, BUT LATER WENT ON TO STUDY GRAPHICS AT LONDON COLLEGE OF PRINTING. AFTER WORKING IN THE MUSIC SCENE, I GOT INTO EDITORIAL DESIGN. I NEVER LEARNED THE RULES OF CORRECT TYPOGRAPHY, WHICH HAS LEFT ME FREE TO DEVELOP MY OWN WORKING METHODS. I HAVE ALSO MADE QUITE A FEW TYPEFACES, LIKE FF BLUR AND TIMES MODERN THAT I DID TOGETHER WITH BEN PRESTON AT RESEARCH STUDIOS. RESEARCH STUDIOS WAS FOUNDED 1994 TOGETHER WITH MY BUSINESS PARTNER FWA RICHARDS. WE'VE GROWN QUITE BIG AND HAVE OPENED OFFICES IN SAN FRANCISCO, PARIS, BERLIN, AND EVEN NEW YORK!

HEATHROW

Neville Brody has designed many different magazines. But what year did he design these different magazines?

WOW! THE CITY LOOKS A BIT LIKE A COMPUTER CHIP!

IT SURE DOES! IN FACT, DURING THE 1980S COMPUTERS ACTUALLY STARTED TO BECOME AVAILABLE FOR GRAPHIC DESIGNERS TO USE IN THEIR WORK. THE IMPACT OF THE COMPUTER WAS ALMOST AS BIG AS WHEN THE STEAM ENGINE WAS INTRODUCED IN THE LATE 1700S. WITH THIS NEW TECHNOLOGY, THERE WERE NO LIMITS TO WHAT GRAPHIC DESIGNERS COULD DO, NO RULES THAT COULDN'T BE BROKEN.

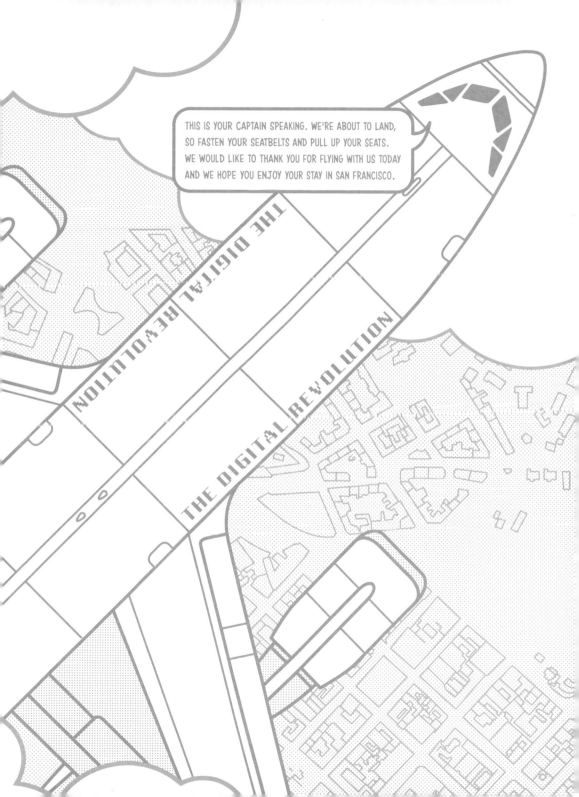

THANKS FOR SHOWING US THIS, SUSAN. NOW KIDDO CAN SEE THE DIFFERENCES BETWEEN NOW AND THEN. YOU KNOW, I USED TO BE A STRIPPER IN MY YOUNGER DAYS.

WHAT!? DOES GRANDMA KNOW!?

223830830
p81/82

1960

Graphic designer

Created the page layouts.

Typesetter

Operated text and typesetting equipment.

Production artist

Pasted all of the elements into position on boards.

Camera operator

Made photographic negatives of the pasteups, art, and photographs.

Stripper

Assembled negatives together.

Platemaker

Prepared the printing plates.

Press operator

Ran the printing presses.

end print
128881841

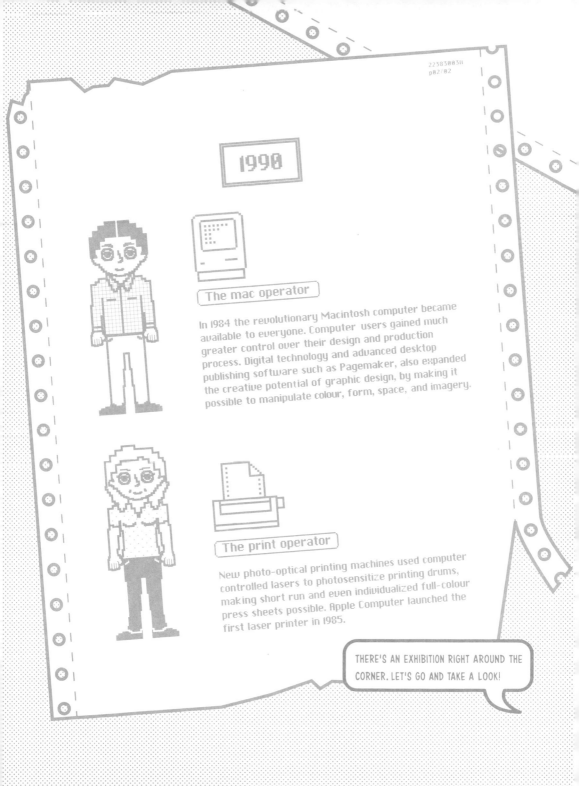

1990

The mac operator

In 1984 the revolutionary Macintosh computer became available to everyone. Computer users gained much greater control over their design and production process. Digital technology and advanced desktop publishing software such as Pagemaker, also expanded the creative potential of graphic design, by making it possible to manipulate colour, form, space, and imagery.

The print operator

New photo-optical printing machines used computer controlled lasers to photosensitize printing drums, making short run and even individualized full-colour press sheets possible. Apple Computer launched the first laser printer in 1985.

THERE'S AN EXHIBITION RIGHT AROUND THE CORNER. LET'S GO AND TAKE A LOOK!

Together with his wife, he founded the design magazine *Emigre* in 1987. *Emigre* presented work and interviews with designers around the world. Along with two other Dutch designers he sought to experiment the new possibilites of the technology. They were criticized by many designers for their extreme experimental methods.

Guess who!

After working as a freelance designer in London, he returned to Berlin in 1979 and founded MetaDesign with his two other partners. In 1989, he and his wife signed contracts with leading type foundries. By taking phone orders and shipping out floppy disks full of digital typefaces, their "FontShop" became the first independent retailer of digital type.

Guess who!

DAVID CARSON
the Father of Grunge

THANKS DUDE! I TOTALLY HATE GRID FORMATS AND CONSISTENT LAYOUTS. INSTEAD, I TRY TO EXPLORE THE EXPRESSIVE POSSIBILITIES OF EACH SUBJECT AND EACH PAGE. I LIKE TO INCLUDE PAGE NUMBERS, SET IN LARGE DISPLAY TYPE AND IMAGES AS PROMINENT DESIGN ELEMENTS IN MY LAYOUTS. OFTEN, I LETTER-SPACE MY ARTICLE TITLES UNPREDICTABLY ACROSS IMAGES OR ARRANGE THEM IN EXPRESSIVE SEQUENCES. I ALSO LIKE TO MAKE MY READER DECIPHER THE MESSAGE BY SLICING AWAY PARTS OF LETTERS. FOR ME, DESIGN IS ALL ABOUT BEING PLAYFUL!

THIS IS SOME QUITE EXPRESSIVE STUFF MR. CARSON!

Which of these statements regarding David Carson are true?

1. In 1989 he was qualified as the 9th best surfer in the world. ◯

2. He was a former sociology teacher. ◯

3. He lost his big toe due to a shark attack. ◯

4. He made the logo for the TV series Baywatch. ◯

Which of these magazines did David Carson work for? Cross out the correct ones.

SIN EAD / O / CON NOR

By using these methods Fred Woodward made a strong visual statement about singer Sinead O'Connor. It was this layout that changed the look and feel of *Rolling Stone* magazine. In other words: nothing compares to this spread.

Fred Woodard became art director at the semi-monthly rock'n roll magazine *Rolling Stone* in 1987. A big turning point was when Woodward reinstated the Oxford rules: multiple lines with thick and thin borders, found in the earlier magazines. Woodward also worked with Gail Anderson on matching typefaces and images to the content, they used a phototypositor to produce hundreds of typefaces. *Rolling Stones* reputation of good editorial and graphic design were well known, so the pressure to maintain their great standards were high. Allthough the magazine converted to Macintosh computers in the early 1990s, Woodward sought a handmade look achieved by type trough a copier many times.

WOW! WHAT A RADICAL WAVE! MY HEAD HURTS! WHERE AM I?

The digital
revolution

Gramps' stuff

SURE! I USE GEOMETRIC REGULATION TO CREATE
AREAS FOR TITLES, SUBTITLES, AND INFORMATION.
THE IMAGES ARE USED AS GUIDES TO HELP VIEW-
ERS AS THEY NAVIGATE THE SITE. IN OPENING
SCREENS FOR EDITORIAL FEATURES, I USE STRIK-
ING IMAGES AND DISCREET TYPOGRAPHY. I FEEL
THAT THIS IS A CONTRAST TO THE MANY OTHER
WEBSITES WITH THEIR MESSY LAYOUTS.

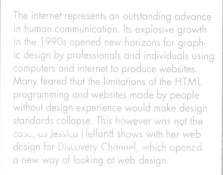

The internet represents an outstanding advance
in human communication. Its explosive growth
in the 1990s opened new horizons for graphic design by professionals and individuals using
computers and internet to produce websites.
Many feared that the limitations of the HTML
programming and websites made by people
without design experience would make design
standards collapse. This however was not the
case, as Jessica Helfand shows with her web
design for Discovery Channel, which opened
a new way of looking at web design.

The graphic design profession was once dom-
inated by a single few individuals. Today, with
an almost universal access to computers, graphic designers appear in big numbers all over the
world. The spreading of the profession did not
only occur through the development of new
computer software and the internet, but also as
a result of both the expansion and increased
quality of design education. And with the spread of the internet graphic design is more international than ever before.

e Man´s Mission for Venom

nie Agita and a
ncrete Slab Named Desir

ve You
med That Plane?

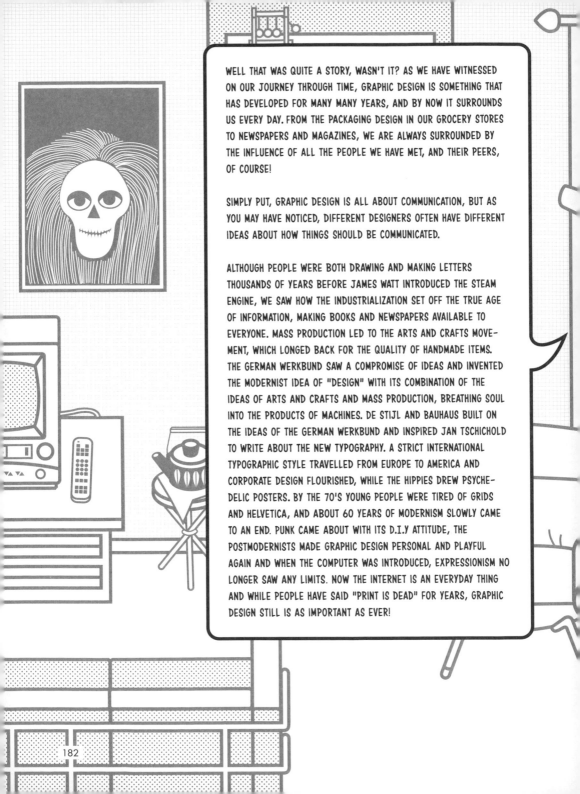

WELL THAT WAS QUITE A STORY, WASN'T IT? AS WE HAVE WITNESSED ON OUR JOURNEY THROUGH TIME, GRAPHIC DESIGN IS SOMETHING THAT HAS DEVELOPED FOR MANY MANY YEARS, AND BY NOW IT SURROUNDS US EVERY DAY. FROM THE PACKAGING DESIGN IN OUR GROCERY STORES TO NEWSPAPERS AND MAGAZINES, WE ARE ALWAYS SURROUNDED BY THE INFLUENCE OF ALL THE PEOPLE WE HAVE MET, AND THEIR PEERS, OF COURSE!

SIMPLY PUT, GRAPHIC DESIGN IS ALL ABOUT COMMUNICATION, BUT AS YOU MAY HAVE NOTICED, DIFFERENT DESIGNERS OFTEN HAVE DIFFERENT IDEAS ABOUT HOW THINGS SHOULD BE COMMUNICATED.

ALTHOUGH PEOPLE WERE BOTH DRAWING AND MAKING LETTERS THOUSANDS OF YEARS BEFORE JAMES WATT INTRODUCED THE STEAM ENGINE, WE SAW HOW THE INDUSTRIALIZATION SET OFF THE TRUE AGE OF INFORMATION, MAKING BOOKS AND NEWSPAPERS AVAILABLE TO EVERYONE. MASS PRODUCTION LED TO THE ARTS AND CRAFTS MOVE- MENT, WHICH LONGED BACK FOR THE QUALITY OF HANDMADE ITEMS. THE GERMAN WERKBUND SAW A COMPROMISE OF IDEAS AND INVENTED THE MODERNIST IDEA OF "DESIGN" WITH ITS COMBINATION OF THE IDEAS OF ARTS AND CRAFTS AND MASS PRODUCTION, BREATHING SOUL INTO THE PRODUCTS OF MACHINES. DE STIJL AND BAUHAUS BUILT ON THE IDEAS OF THE GERMAN WERKBUND AND INSPIRED JAN TSCHICHOLD TO WRITE ABOUT THE NEW TYPOGRAPHY. A STRICT INTERNATIONAL TYPOGRAPHIC STYLE TRAVELLED FROM EUROPE TO AMERICA AND CORPORATE DESIGN FLOURISHED, WHILE THE HIPPIES DREW PSYCHE- DELIC POSTERS. BY THE 70'S YOUNG PEOPLE WERE TIRED OF GRIDS AND HELVETICA, AND ABOUT 60 YEARS OF MODERNISM SLOWLY CAME TO AN END. PUNK CAME ABOUT WITH ITS D.I.Y ATTITUDE, THE POSTMODERNISTS MADE GRAPHIC DESIGN PERSONAL AND PLAYFUL AGAIN AND WHEN THE COMPUTER WAS INTRODUCED, EXPRESSIONISM NO LONGER SAW ANY LIMITS. NOW THE INTERNET IS AN EVERYDAY THING AND WHILE PEOPLE HAVE SAID "PRINT IS DEAD" FOR YEARS, GRAPHIC DESIGN STILL IS AS IMPORTANT AS EVER!

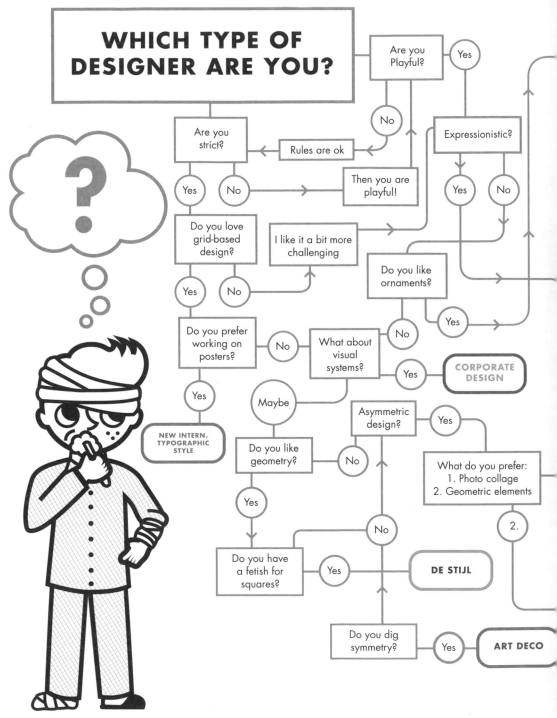

WHICH TYPE OF DESIGNER ARE YOU?

Are you Playful? — Yes

No

Are you strict? ← Rules are ok

Then you are playful!

Expressionistic? — Yes / No

Yes / No

Do you love grid-based design? — Yes / No

I like it a bit more challenging

Do you like ornaments? — No / Yes

Do you prefer working on posters? — No — What about visual systems? — Yes — **CORPORATE DESIGN**

Yes

Maybe

Asymmetric design? — Yes

NEW INTERN. TYPOGRAPHIC STYLE

Do you like geometry? — No

What do you prefer:
1. Photo collage
2. Geometric elements

No

2.

Yes

Do you have a fetish for squares? — Yes — **DE STIJL**

Do you dig symmetry? — Yes — **ART DECO**

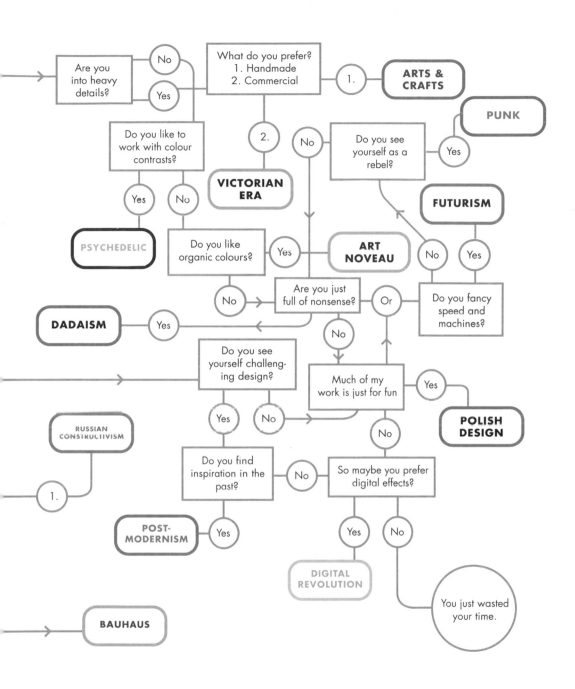

Are you into heavy details?

No → What do you prefer?
1. Handmade
2. Commercial

Yes

1. → **ARTS & CRAFTS**

2. → **VICTORIAN ERA**

No → Do you see yourself as a rebel?

Yes → **PUNK**

No → **FUTURISM**

Yes → Do you fancy speed and machines?

Do you like to work with colour contrasts?

Yes → **PSYCHEDELIC**

No → Do you like organic colours?

Yes → **ART NOVEAU**

No → Are you just full of nonsense?

Yes → **DADAISM**

No → Much of my work is just for fun

Or

Do you see yourself challenging design?

Yes → Do you find inspiration in the past?

No → So maybe you prefer digital effects?

RUSSIAN CONSTRUCTIVISM

1.

Yes → **POST-MODERNISM**

Yes → **POLISH DESIGN**

Yes → **DIGITAL REVOLUTION**

No → You just wasted your time.

BAUHAUS

AMSTERDAM

OSLO

BOOKS WE HAVE USED AND RECOMMEND FOR FURTHER READING:

PHILIP B. MEGGS & ALSTON W. PURVIS –
MEGGS' HISTORY OF GRAPHIC DESIGN
PHIL BAINES – *PENGUIN BY DESIGN*
WILLIAM SMOCK – *BAUHAUS IDEAL THEN AND NOW*
RICHARD HOLLIS – *GRAPHIC DESIGN: A CONCISE HISTORY*
STEPHEN J. ESKILSON – *GRAPHIC DESIGN: A NEW HISTORY*
SEIBUNDO SHINKOSHA CO – *SAUL BASS AND ASSOCIATES*
KERRY WILLIAM PURCEL – *ALEXEY BRODOVITCH*

THE KIND OF ARCTIC PAPER THAT HAS
BEEN USED IN THIS BOOK:

P. 1–192 MUNKEN LYNX ROUGH 120G

FOR THE CUT-OUT PAGES,
MUNKEN LYNX 200G WAS USED.

AND A BIG
SHOUT-OUT TO
WIKIPEDIA.ORG
AS WELL!

FOR THE ANSWERS CHECK OUT:
GRAPHICDESIGNFORRAINYDAYS.COM

AND FOR MORE INFORMATION:
STUDIO3.NO

Kristofer Haugvik

Sofie Platou

Mikael Fløysand

Catherine Sagaute

CUT IT OUT!

My **FAVOURITE** TEA

GRAMP & KIDDO'S BISCUITS FOR SWEETIES

GRAMP'S LUXURY MARMALADE

HELVETICA
Hoffmann&Miedinger

MELIOR
Hermann Zapf

ALDUS
Hermann Zapf

AKZIDENZ GROTESK
H. Berthold AG Typefoundry

PALATINO
Hermann Zapf

EGYPTIENNE
Adrian Frutiger

OPTIMA
Hermann Zapf

UNIVERS
Adrian Frutiger

QUESTION

Privat Livemont made the famous absinthe posters, highly inspired by Muchas work. But it was one thing that he invented in poster design. What was that?

A. Repetition of the main figure that created layers.

B. A white thick contour around the main figures.

C. The decorated board around the poster.

QUESTION

Van de Velde thought that art, painting, graphic design, industrial design, and architecture shared a common language of form and that all are equally important to the community.

True or False?

QUESTION

In the Netherlands art noveau was called Nieuwe Kunst, but between which years did it exist?

A. 1930-1940

B. 1870-1950

C. 1892-1906

QUESTION

Where was Jan Toorop born and what inspired him from his childhood that could be seen in his work?

A. He was born on Java and was inspired by the Javanese wajang shadow puppets.

B. He was born in Norway and was inpired by the Norwegian folklore patterns.

C. He was born in Paris and was inspired by Muchas work.

QUESTION

When art noveau came to Germany, the style was named after a magazine that began publication in Munich, 1896. What was the name of the magazine and the style?

A. Mucha and Muchastyle

B. Jugend and Jugendstil

C. Liberty and Style Liberty

QUESTION

Designers in Germany, Scotland, and Austria moved from the floral phase of art nouveau towards another approach. What was the new approach?

A. A geometric approach

B. A medieval approach

C. An organic approach

QUESTION

Jugend magazine had a specific editorial approach to their cover on every issue, what was that?

A. They had a new designer each week that designed the cover with matching masthead.

B. It was the same motive on the cover but created by a different artist each week.

C. The masthead was the same each week.

QUESTION

Which was the first German Type Foundry to release Otto Eckmann's Eckmannschrift in 1900?

A. The Boston Type Foundry

B. Thorne's Fann Street Foundry

C. The Klingspor Foundry

QUESTION

For which publisher did Peter Behrens make this trademark?

A. Der Bunte Vogel

B. Insel Verlag

C. Eckmann Schriftprobe

answer

C. 1892– 1906

answer

TRUE

answer

B. A white thick contour around the main figures.

answer

A. A geometric approach

answer

B. Jugend and jugendstil

answer

A. He was born on Java and was inspired by the Javanese wajang shadow puppets.

answer

B. Insel Verlag

answer

C. The Klingspor Foundry

answer

A. They had a new designer each week that designed the cover with matching masthead.

FONDAZIONE E MANIFESTO

DEL

FUTURISMO

(Pubblicato dal " FIGARO „ di Parigi il 20 Febbraio 1909)

1. We want to sing the love of danger, the habit of energy and rashness.

2. The essential elements of our poetry will be courage, audacity and revolt.

3. Literature has up to now magnified pensive immobility, ecstasy and slumber. We want to exalt movements of aggression, feverish sleeplessness, the double march, the perilous leap, the slap and the blow with the fist.

4. We declare that the splendor of the world has been enriched by a new beauty: the beauty of speed. A racing automobile with its bonnet adorned with great tubes like serpents with explosive breath ... a roaring motor car, which seems to run on machine-gun fire, is more beautiful than the Victory of Samothrace.

5. We want to sing the man at the wheel, the ideal axis of which crosses the earth, itself hurled along its orbit.

6. The poet must spend himself with warmth, glamour and prodigality to increase the enthusiastic fervor of the primordial elements.

7. Beauty exists only in struggle. There is no masterpiece that has not an aggressive character. Poetry must be a violent assault on the forces of the unknown, to force them to bow before man.

8. We are on the extreme promontory of the centuries! What is the use of looking behind at the moment when we must open the mysterious shutters of the impossible? Time and Space died yesterday. We are already living in the absolute, since we have already created eternal, omnipresent speed.

9. We want to glorify war — the only cure for the world — militarism, patriotism, the destructive gesture of the anarchists, the beautiful ideas which kill, and contempt for woman.

10. We want to demolish museums and libraries, fight morality, feminism and all opportunist and utilitarian cowardice.

11. We will sing of the great crowds agitated by work, pleasure and revolt; the multi-coloured and polyphonic surf of revolutions in modern capitals: the nocturnal vibration of the arsenals and the workshops beneath their violent electric moons: the gluttonous railway stations devouring smoking serpents; factories suspended from the clouds by the thread of their smoke; bridges with the leap of gymnasts flung across the diabolic cutlery of sunny rivers: adventurous steamers sniffing the horizon; great-breasted locomotives, puffing on the rails like enormous steel horses with long tubes for bridle, and the gliding flight of aeroplanes whose propeller sounds like the flapping of a flag and the applause of enthusiastic crowds.

BAUHAUS

HOCHSCHULE FÜR GESTALTUNG

DIPLOMA

You have satisfactorily completed a course of study at the Bauhaus
Houchschule für Design and are therefore awarded this Diploma.

WALTER GROPIUS
PRINCIPAL

YOUR SIGNATURE

Cut out and place
around a small
take-away cup!

first things first

A manifesto

We, the undersigned, are graphic designers, photographers and students who have been brought up in a world in which the techniques and apparatus of advertising have persistently been presented to us as the most lucrative, effective and desirable means of using our talents. We have been bombarded with publications devoted to this belief, applauding the work of those who have flogged their skill and imagination to sell such things as:

cat food, stomach powders, detergent, hair restorer, striped toothpaste, after-shave lotion, beforeshave lotion, slim-ming diets, fattening diets, deodorants, fizzy water, cigarettes, roll-ons, pull-ons and slip-ons.

By far the greatest effort of those work-ing in the advertising industry are wasted on these trivial purposes, which contri-bute little or nothing to our national prosperity.

In common with an increasing numer of the general public, we have reached a saturation point at which the high pitch-ed scream of consumer selling is no more than sheer noise. We think that there are other things more worth using our skill and experience on. There are signs for streets and buildings, books and periodicals, catalogues, instructional manuals, industrial photography, educa-tional aids, films, television features, scientific and industrial publications and all the other media through which we promote our trade, our education, our culture and our greater awareness of the world.

We do not advocate the abolition of high pressure consumer advertising: this is not feasible. Nor do we want to take any of the fun out of life. But we are proposing a reversal of priorities in favour of the more useful and more lasting forms of communication.

We hope that our society will tire of gimmick merchants, status salesmen and hidden persuaders, and that the prior call on our skills will be for worth-while purposes. With this in mind we propose to share our experience and opinions, and to make them available to colleagues, students and others who may be interested.

*Published by Ken Garland
in January 1964*

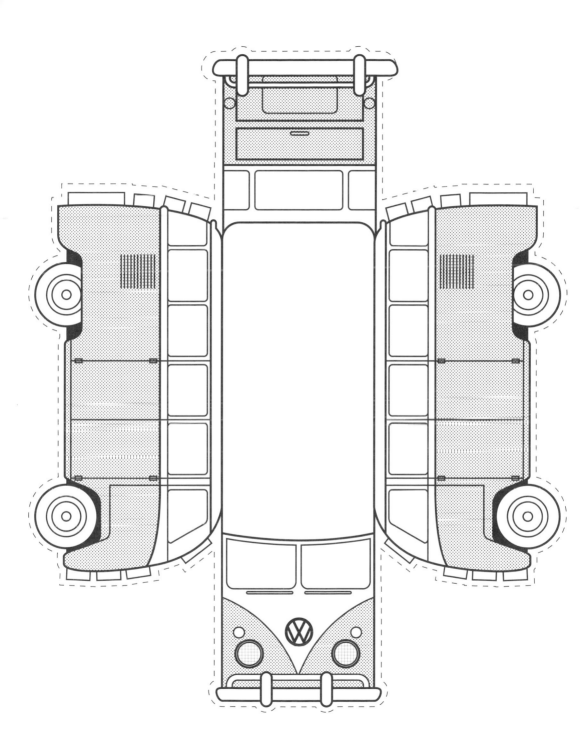

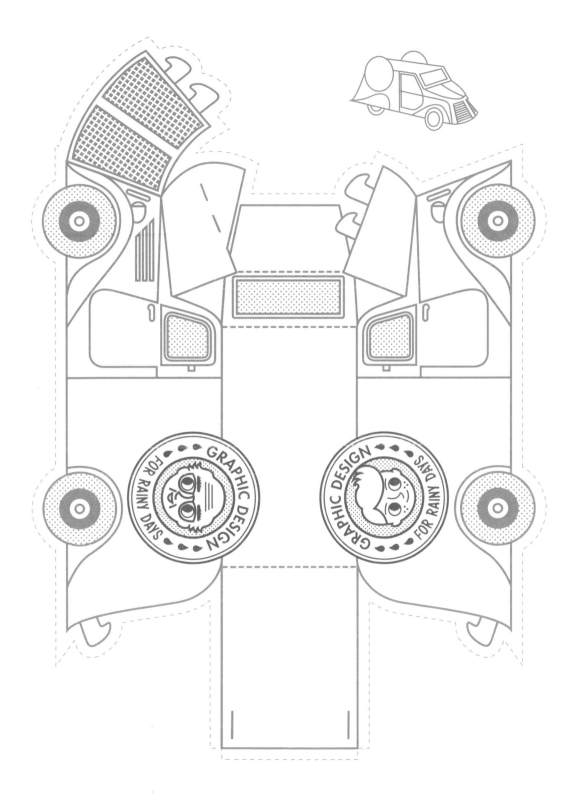

GRAPHIC DESIGN • FOR RAINY DAYS

GRAPHIC DESIGN • FOR RAINY DAYS

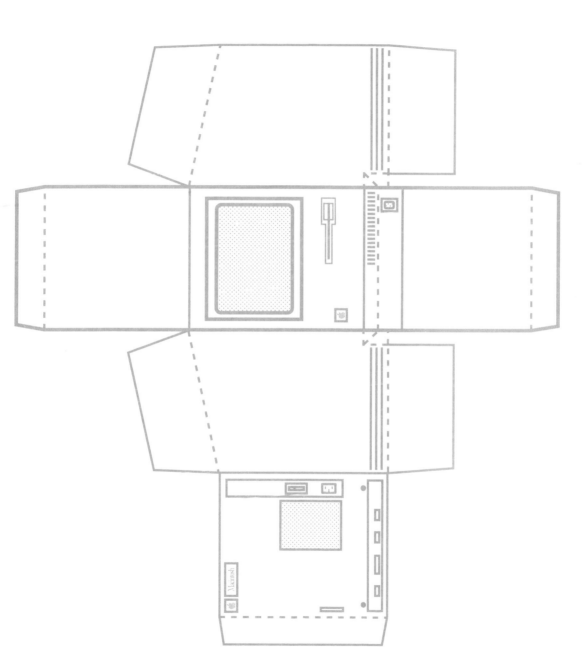

Cut out your favorite designer!

FOLD

FOLD

FOLD

FOLD

FOLD

FOLD

Louis Prang, was an American printer, lithographer and publisher. He is known as the father of the American Christmas card.

William Morris, (1834 – 1896) was an English textile designer, artist, writer, and pioneer in the Arts and Crafts Movement. Best known for his botanical patterns and ornaments.

Henri de Toulouse-Lautrec. Broke new ground when it came to poster design with his use of symbolic shaped and communicative images.

GLUE TO BACK
FOLD

GLUE TO BACK
FOLD

GLUE TO BACK
FOLD

Cut out your favorite designer!

FOLD

FOLD

FOLD

FOLD

FOLD

FOLD

Johannes Itten,
(1888-1967) was a
Swiss painter, designer,
and teacher. Well
known for colour
studies. One of the
many important
teachers of Bauhaus.

John Heartfield,
turned out to be highly
active in the Dada
movement. He is
famous for his satirising
photomontage posters
in World War II.

Jan Tschichold
(1902-1974) a master
typographer, book
designer, teacher, and
writer. A leading
founder in The New
Typography movement
and fighter for the
asymmetric typography.

GLUE TO BACK
FOLD

GLUE TO BACK
FOLD

GLUE TO BACK
FOLD

Cut out your favorite designer!

FOLD

FOLD

FOLD

FOLD

FOLD

FOLD

Josef Müller Brockmann (1914 – 1996) swiss designer known for his simple designs, clean use of typography, and grids. A pioneer in Swiss design.

Saul Bass, lived between 1920 and 1996. American graphic designer known for motion picture title sequences.

Paul Rand, (1914 – 1996) an American graphic designer, best known for his corporate identities.

GLUE TO BACK
FOLD

GLUE TO BACK
FOLD

GLUE TO BACK
FOLD

Cut out your favorite designer!

FOLD

FOLD

FOLD

FOLD

FOLD

FOLD

Stanley Mouse.
Born in 1940. Known for his psychedelic rock posters for the *Grateful Dead*. Was one of the artist in "The great five".

Rosmarie Tissi.
Austrian designer. Worked together with Siegfried Odermatt and is known for postmodern works in a playful and intuitive manner.

David Carson.
also known as the Father of Grunge was perhaps the most influential graphic designer of the nineties with experimental use of layouts and typography.

FOLD
GLUE TO BACK

FOLD
GLUE TO BACK

FOLD
GLUE TO BACK

A HISTORY OF GRAPHIC DESIGN
FOR RAINY DAYS

BY STUDIO 3

Project management by Julian Sorge for Gestalten
Production management by Martin Bretschneider for Gestalten
Proofreading by Leina Gonzalez Baird
Printed by Graphicom, Vicenza
Made in Europe

Published by Gestalten, Berlin 2011
ISBN 978-3-89955-389-5

For more information, please visit www.gestalten.com.

Bibliographic information published by the Deutsche Nationalbibliothek. The Deutsche Nationalbibliothek lists this publication in the Deutsche Nationalbibliografie; detailed bibliographic data are available online at http://dnb.d-nb.de.

This book was printed according to the internationally ac-
cepted ISO 14001 standards for environmental protection,
which specify requirements for an environmental management
system.

This book was printed on paper certified by the FSC®.

Mixed Sources
Product group from well-managed
forests, controlled sources and
recycled wood or fibre
FSC   www.fsc.org Cert no. CQ-COC-000015
© 1996 Forest Stewardship Council

Gestalten is a climate-neutral company. We collaborate with
the non-profit carbon offset provider myclimate www.
myclimate.org to neutralize the company's carbon footprint
produced through our worldwide business activities by invest-
ing in projects that reduce CO_2 emissions www.gestalten.com/
myclimate.

myclimate
Protect our planet